Low-Risk Futures Trading

A Structured Guide to Strategy, Psychology, and Risk Management

Nadia Karim

BengalGeek

Published by BengalGeek™ LLC: www.bengalgeek.com

Disclaimer Notice:

This book is provided for educational and informational purposes only. Every effort has been made to ensure the accuracy, reliability, and completeness of the information presented at the time of publication. However, no guarantees or warranties, expressed or implied, are made regarding the accuracy or completeness of the content.

The author and publisher are not financial advisors, brokers, or licensed investment professionals. The information in this book should not be considered financial, investment, legal, or professional advice. Trading futures, options, and other financial instruments involves substantial risk and may not be suitable for all individuals. Readers are encouraged to conduct independent research and consult qualified professionals before making financial or trading decisions.

By reading this book, the reader acknowledges and agrees that the author and publisher shall not be held responsible for any direct or indirect losses, damages, or consequences resulting from the application or misuse of the information contained within this publication, including but not limited to trading losses, financial decisions, errors, omissions, or inaccuracies.

LOW-RISK FUTURES TRADING

Contents

Introduction

If you have picked up this book, most likely you are seeking financial freedom through a side hustle while maintaining a regular job, or you are hoping to better understand whether you should start a side hustle through futures trading to earn additional income. Rest assured, you are in the right place.

I will guide you through each chapter, drawing on thorough research and accurate information, all grounded in personal experience and real-life endeavors. Look out for the light bulb symbol for special emphasis and practical example tips. The first three chapters begin by covering essential trading fundamentals and psychology applicable to all forms of trading.

However, the latter chapters focus specifically on futures trading, offering insights and practical guidance to help you navigate this lucrative market segment. My goal is to support you at every stage, making trading accessible and enjoyable regardless of your level of knowledge or financial background.

Who This Book Is For

This book is for working professionals, busy parents, and motivated beginners who want to build a reliable side income through futures trading without sacrificing career stability or personal responsibilities. It is designed for readers who value structure, emotional discipline, and low-risk decision-making, rather than gambling or high-stress speculation.

Whether you are a complete beginner, or someone returning to the markets after setbacks, or a trader seeking a more organized and sustainable approach, this guide provides the clarity, confidence, and practical tools you need to trade successfully within a real-world schedule. When I first began trading, I did not have the advantage of financial abundance.

I faced the emotional and financial instability of a marriage where household expenses were not shared fairly, and even after separation, financial support for my shared-custody child remained inconsistent and unreliable. These circumstances deeply influenced my approach to the market. I sometimes made decisions that resulted in losses, and when your financial foundation is shaky, your trading emotions become more intense.

A losing trade does not feel like a minor setback; it feels deeply personal. A winning trade can seem more like relief than a testament to your skill. This reality influenced every aspect of my trading plan. That is why I am extremely passionate about spreading financial literacy for successful Side Hustle Trading and about sharing my experiences and mistakes along the way so you do not go through the same situations.

One of the greatest challenges in trading psychology is learning to manage our instinctive emotional responses to market changes. Fear of loss may cause you to hesitate or make impulsive choices, while greed can cloud your judgment and push you toward unnecessary risks. Uncertainty about where the market is heading often produces anxiety and makes it harder to choose wisely.

To move past these emotional roadblocks, traders must intentionally build emotional resilience and find strategies that work for them. This could involve practicing mindfulness, reframing negative thoughts, and maintaining a balanced outlook on both wins and losses. It is vital to maintain discipline and consistency in your trading practices for successful self-management.

This means following a well-crafted trading plan, setting achievable goals, and making thoughtful decisions at every step. These are the main pillars of this book: developing the right mindset for trading, mastering the fundamentals, and engaging with futures markets from a place of knowledge so that trading feels less intimidating and more rewarding.

As you progress through the chapters, you will find:

- Common trading knowledge (first 3 chapters)
- Clear explanations of futures markets
- Practical trading frameworks
- Risk management guidance

How to Get the Most Out of This Book

This book is your gateway to the knowledge and tools you need to embark on this journey of learning about Sid Hustle Trading and Futures confidently. Use this checklist as your roadmap to learn efficiently, stay organized, and apply each concept with confidence.

Read the Chapters in Order

For the best learning experience with this book, we recommend following the chapters in order. This method enables you to develop a strong grasp of Side Hustle Trading, beginning with basic principles and advancing to more complex strategies. Each chapter offers valuable insights and practical guidance designed to enhance your trading skills. This book is designed to make trading structured and accessible, regardless of your starting knowledge.

Use a Trading Logbook

Record every trade documenting your reasoning, emotions, results, and lessons. Growth in trading comes from review, not from the trade itself. Throughout their book, there will be multiple reminders to use the Trading Success Logbookpublished by BengalGeek™.

Define Your Personal Goals

Before diving into strategies, clarify what you want from trading, which may include income, skill development, or long-term growth. This book helps to dive deeper into defining one's trading goals. Make sure to set up enough time regularly to go through the concepts outlined in this book.

Match Strategies to Your Schedule

Choose approaches that fit your real life; specifically understand your primary job, family responsibilities, and available time. There are chapters that will go deeper into the psychology of time management in detail.

Practice Before You Risk Capital

Use paper trading or micro contracts to build confidence and consistency before scaling up. Map out the plan and practice mock trading before taking actual steps.

Review Weekly and Monthly

Review your trading plans and executed trades regularly. Consistency compounds. Evaluate your performance, identify patterns, and refine your plan.

Focus on Psychology as Much as Strategy

Your mindset drives your results. Revisit the psychology and risk management chapters whenever emotions start influencing decisions.

Use the Appendices and References

These sections provide tools, definitions, and resources to deepen your understanding.

Avoid Skipping Ahead to "Advanced" Sections

The book expects the readers to take actions with the knowledge learned from this book. There is an advanced techniques chapter towards the end. Advanced techniques are powerful, but only when built on a solid foundation.

Apply One Concept at a Time

We learn by doing. However, do not overwhelm yourself trying to master all the skills outlined in this book all at once. Master one skill before adding another.

Look for the Light Bulb Sign

Look for the light bulb icon throughout the book to find practical examples and insights designed to help you maximize learning in each chapter.

Continue Your Learning Journey

By building strong routines and clear structures, you can reduce the influence of emotional swings and remain focused on your long-term objectives. Finding a healthy balance between your trading life, professional duties, and personal well-being is just as important. Your trading plan should always reflect your own unique circumstances. I am a single mother working full-time in a structured corporate environment.

My income remained steady, but my financial flexibility was limited. I continued to invest in my professional growth while simultaneously managing all household responsibilities. Taking time for activities outside of trading, like exercise, hobbies, or simply cherishing moments with loved ones, helps relieve stress and protects you from burnout, ultimately supporting both your mental and emotional health.

If you find this book helpful, I encourage you to explore additional publications, resources, and educational materials available at bengalgeek.com. You can also scan the QR code below for quick access. Do not forget to explore other side hustle books in the series to broaden your knowledge and skill set.

SCAN ME

Your feedback and support truly make a difference. If this book has helped you gain clarity, confidence, or practical trading knowledge, please consider leaving a review. Reviews not only support future editions and projects but also help other readers discover valuable trading resources.

Chapter One

All About Side Hustle Trading

"The intelligent investor is a realist who sells to optimists and buys from pessimists." – Benjamin Graham

In today's financial landscape, the concept of a side hustle has become a powerful way to supplement income and build financial independence. Side Hustle Trading embodies the fusion of entrepreneurial spirit and financial acumen. Extra income can create options like building savings, investing in personal growth, funding experiences, or even treating yourself to a weekend getaway. By refining your strategies with real-time data and observations, you can improve your returns in the dynamic world of investing.

The additional income from Side Hustle Trading can open up a world of possibilities. However, success does not come from chasing quick gains. It comes from continuous education, emotional discipline, structured risk management, consistent execution, trading rewards preparation, not impulse.

What is Side Hustle Trading?

Side Hustle Trading entails the proactive engagement in financial markets, be it stocks, forex, cryptocurrencies, commodities, or derivatives, concurrently with one's primary source of income. What distinguishes Side Hustle Trading from traditional investing paradigms is its inherent flexibility and agility, empowering individuals to navigate market fluctuations, capitalize on emerging trends, and unlock the potential for swift returns. And who doesn't like the extra cash in the pocket?

Unlike traditional long-term investing, Side Hustle Trading emphasizes flexibility. It allows individuals to respond to market opportunities, manage risk strategically, and generate additional income without leaving their full-time job. When approached with discipline, trading becomes more than a money-making activity; it becomes a skill-based pursuit rooted in strategy, psychology, and risk management.

Venturing into trading may seem daunting, but it is a chance to develop valuable skills and broaden your mindset. Pitfalls such as overtrading, emotional bias, and insufficient research pose significant hurdles that traders must navigate with prudence and discipline (*Nomadic Millennial, n.d.; Keegan Edwards, n.d.*).

This book focuses specifically on Futures Trading as a side hustle. While trading may appear complex or intimidating, it can be structured, learnable, and systematic when approached correctly. Futures trading offers extended market hours, defined contracts, and leverage, making it attractive for individuals balancing professional commitments.

Benefits of Side Hustle Trading

Through committed practice and continuous education, individuals refine not only their financial skills but also nurture resilience, adaptability, and a mindset conducive to progress. This philosophy offers individuals a platform to challenge themselves, explore new frontiers, and realize their fullest capabilities within the ever-evolving landscape of financial markets.

1. Flexibility and Independence

Side Hustle Traders allocate a few hours a day to engage in trading activities, allowing for the exploration of market opportunities while balancing other commitments (*Market Rebellion, n.d.*). Futures markets offer extended hours, enabling traders to engage in put sales and capitalize on market movements even after their regular working hours. This flexibility allows you to build a second income stream without sacrificing career stability.

2. Income Potential

One of the primary attractions of Side Hustle Trading is the potential for significant financial gains. Stock trading, for example, offers individuals the opportunity to generate substantial profits through prudent investment decisions and effective risk management (*MyEspresso, n.d.*).

Forex trading as a side hustle also presents opportunities for profit-making, although it requires understanding the complexities of the foreign exchange market and managing currency fluctuations effectively (*Insights Success, n.d.*). With sound research and disciplined execution, trading can generate meaningful returns. While profits are never guaranteed, structured decision-making and proper risk control create the conditions for consistent performance.

3. Skill Development

Engaging in Side Hustle Trading helps acquire valuable financial skills and market knowledge. Trading provides an opportunity to learn and apply fundamental concepts such as technical analysis, risk management, and portfolio diversification (*Skillsuccess, n.d*.).

Trading builds valuable skills such as

- Technical and Fundamental Analysis

- Risk Assessment
- Capital Allocation
- Emotional Regulation
- Decision-Making Under Pressure

Challenges of Side Hustle Trading

Engaging in Side Hustle Trading endeavors unveils a realm of financial prospects, yet it also introduces a diverse array of obstacles that necessitate meticulous navigation and thoughtful strategizing.

Let's explore the key challenges identified across various sources and discuss strategies to overcome them:

1. Time Management

One of the most significant challenges of Side Hustle Trading is balancing trading activities with other professional and personal commitments. Traders often struggle to allocate sufficient time for research, analysis, and monitoring of market trends amid their busy schedules.

The demands of full-time employment or other obligations can impede traders' ability to stay up to date on market developments and make informed trading decisions. To address this challenge, traders must prioritize tasks, establish a structured trading routine, and leverage tools and technology to streamline their trading processes (*Forex4you, n.d.*).

2. Emotional Discipline

The volatile nature of financial markets can trigger emotional responses such as fear, greed, and anxiety, potentially leading to impulsive decisions and losses. It's crucial to maintain emotional equilibrium and stick to predefined trading strategies, even during the busiest work hours.

Cultivating discipline through mindfulness practices, journaling in the Trading Success Logbook, and seeking support from mentorship or trading communities can help traders stay focused and disciplined (*Coinmonks, n.d.*). Remember, your regular job provides stability while your Side Hustle Trading habits grow. Keeping the two separate requires a strong and disciplined mind, but the rewards can be substantial.

3. Market Volatility

The unpredictable nature of market fluctuations can result in rapid price movements and unexpected outcomes. Sudden geopolitical events, economic indicators, and regulatory changes can significantly impact asset prices and disrupt trading strategies.

To navigate market volatility effectively, traders must stay informed, adapt to changing market conditions, and exercise caution during periods of heightened uncertainty (*Everand, n.d.*). Adaptability and preparation are essential.

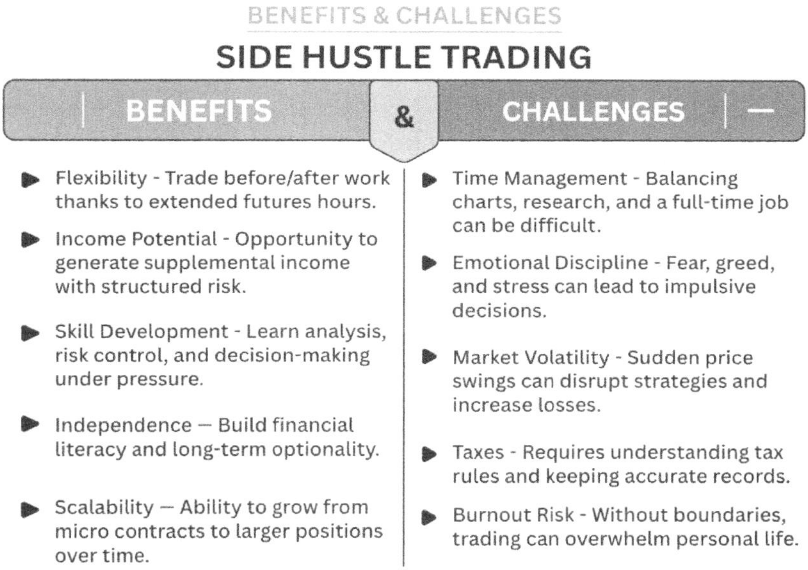

Figure 1.1: Side Hustle Trading - Benefits vs Challenges

Other Considerations

Previously, we discussed the challenges and limitations one may face towards trading. In this section, we are highlighting other practical considerations for a trader.

1. Time Commitment

As a general guideline, individuals engaging in futures trading as a side hustle may allocate at least 1-2 hours per day for market analysis and research. This time can be used to review the following:

- Price Chart review
- Study Technical indicators
- Stay updated on relevant news and economic developments.
- Strategy evaluation

However, traders need to find a balance between their trading activities and other commitments to avoid burnout and maintain a healthy lifestyle. Additionally, traders should continuously assess their strategies and adjust their time commitment based on their evolving trading goals, market conditions, and personal preferences. Trading should enhance your life, not consume it.

2. Capital Requirements

Investopedia suggests that technically, one can commence trading with as little as $100, but such a meager amount is impractical due to the high-risk nature of futures markets. The TradePro Academy underscores the significance of choosing a reputable broker, which directly impacts the capital requirements.

However, The Motley Fool emphasizes the necessity of a realistic capital cushion, advising traders to start with a minimum of $2,500 to $7,500, fostering resilience against market volatility and potential losses. Brokers may stipulate different minimum deposits, with ranges spanning from $500 to $5,000 or more contingent on the platform's requirements.

While some brokers allow small deposits, futures trading requires realistic capital to withstand volatility. Consequently, the capital needed encompasses not only the brokerage minimums but also an ample buffer to navigate the inherent risks of trading.

By investing more, individuals can potentially earn higher returns, as larger capital allows for greater flexibility in trading strategies and the ability to capitalize on market opportunities with larger positions. Therefore, a practical starting range for many traders is between $2,500 and $7,500.

Most importantly, never trade money you cannot afford to lose. Capital should include both trading funds and a reserve buffer. The goal is to achieve this objective with patience and understanding that steady investment is needed. This approach helps traders avoid impulsive decisions driven by emotions, ensuring a disciplined and strategic approach to their trading journey.

3. Taxes

Generally, profits from futures trading are subject to capital gains taxation worldwide. This tax is levied on the net profits earned from selling futures contracts, calculated by subtracting the purchase price from the selling price.

The capital gains tax rate fluctuates based on factors such as your income, the duration you held the contracts, and whether the gains are categorized as short-term or long-term. Short-term gains, arising from contracts held for less than a year, often face higher tax rates.

Moreover, specific deductions and tax credits for futures trading might be available, contingent upon local tax regulations. Seeking guidance from a tax professional specializing in investment taxation is recommended to ensure compliance and enhance tax efficiency in your futures trading endeavors.

Figure 1.2: Taxes on Futures Trading Profits

Chapter Summary

In this introductory chapter, we introduced Side Hustle Trading as a structured way to generate supplemental income while maintaining career stability. By embracing adaptability, developing skills, and handling risks wisely, individuals can position themselves strategically to seize the numerous opportunities presented by Side Hustle Trading. This sets them on a path towards financial empowerment and sustained prosperity, marking a transformative journey.

Side Hustle Trading requires preparation, emotional control, and ongoing refinement. With structure and consistency, it can become a powerful tool for financial growth. The next chapter will begin building the methodical plan required to navigate Side Hustle Trading and futures markets with clarity and confidence.

Chapter Two

Building a Side Hustle Trading Plan

"Invest for the long haul. Don't get too greedy and don't get too scared." - Shelby M.C. Davis

In the dynamic landscape of finance and entrepreneurship, venturing into a side hustle in the low-risk Futures Market may seem daunting. However, with a well-crafted plan and execution, it can pave the way for success. As Benjamin Franklin famously said, *"By failing to prepare, you are preparing to fail."* In this chapter, we explore how building a clear and disciplined trading plan can strengthen your journey toward financial independence and long-term wealth creation.

Why a Trading Plan Matters

Crafting a trading plan serves as a strategic blueprint, outlining objectives, trading strategies, and risk management protocols.

Without a plan, trading becomes reactive. With a plan, it becomes intentional and structured. In today's world of finance and maintaining a day job with a structured schedule, creating a Side Hustle Trading plan is essential for those looking to expand their income options and delve into financial markets.

A trading plan provides clarity and accountability, and the components are laid out below:

1. Your Financial Goals

Firstly, defining clear objectives provides a roadmap for traders, helping them focus their efforts and resources toward specific financial goals. Your trading plan should highlight your financial goals, risk tolerance, and time commitments (*Think Markets, n.d.*).

Whether the aim is to generate supplemental income to support existing earnings or to build a robust investment portfolio for long-term wealth accumulation, clearly articulated objectives provide clarity and direction in navigating the complexities of the financial markets.

2. Your Trading Approach

Secondly, a robust trading strategy outlines the approach you will take to enter and exit trades, manage risk, and capitalize on market opportunities. Your trading strategy should include criteria for trade entry, trade exit, and risk management (*IG, 2022*).

This involves meticulous research, analysis, and decision-making processes to identify trading opportunities, determine entry and exit points, and manage risk effectively. A well-defined trading strategy enables traders to capitalize on market trends, leverage their strengths, and mitigate potential losses, thereby increasing the likelihood of achieving their financial objectives over time.

3. Your Risk Tolerance

Thirdly, determine the maximum amount of capital you are willing to risk on each trade and establish predefined risk-reward ratios to guide your decision-making process. By implementing robust risk management measures, you can protect your investment capital and minimize the impact of adverse market movements on your trading account. Risk management measures should include setting stop-loss orders, diversifying your portfolio, and limiting the size of individual trades (*Investopedia, 2004*).

4. Monitor Performance

Keeping detailed records of your trades allows you to analyze your trading patterns, identify strengths and weaknesses, and refine your trading strategies accordingly (*Nadex, n.d.*). Regularly review your trading activities, assess your performance metrics, and identify areas for improvement, which can be done just by spending a few hours per day.

Additionally, seek feedback from experienced traders, participate in trading communities, and stay updated on market developments to enhance your trading skills and knowledge. We highly encourage using the Trading Success Logbookto track your trading activities systematically, which can provide valuable insights and help you improve your trading skills over time.

Figure 2.1: Monitoring Trading Performance

Practical Trading Plan

Your trading plan should not be just a set of abstract rules. It needs to fit into your everyday life and consider your personal circumstances. Think of it like planning a trip; you would not book a whirlwind tour if you have young children and a demanding job; you would plan something that realistically fits your schedule and energy levels. Similarly, your trading plan must align with your real-world responsibilities and lifestyle. We'll look at how this works in practice.

1. Your Financial Goals

Your goals determine how you behave in the market. As a single parent with a stable job, my goal was rarely aggressive wealth acceleration.

It was more:

- Supplemental Income
- Skill Development
- Capital Preservation
- Gradual Account Growth

For example, instead of saying, "I want to double my account in three months," a more realistic goal might be, "I want to grow my account by 3–5% per month while protecting capital." Or even: "For the first six months, my goal is learning consistency, not profits." When financial responsibilities are significant, such as mortgage, childcare, education, and emergency savings, your trading goal must prioritize stability over excitement. Clear goals provide direction during volatile market periods.

2. Your Trading Approach

Your lifestyle determines your strategy. As a full-time professional and a single mom busy with kids' extracurricular duties and no help, I did not have the luxury of watching charts all day. My trading approach had to be structured and included the following:

- Early Morning Analysis
- Evening Review
- Predefined Setups
- Alerts during Work Hours

For example, instead of trading five times a day, I might decide, "I will take only one high-quality breakout setup per week." Clarity reduces emotional decision-making. Your approach should be simple, repeatable, and manageable within your schedule.

3. Your Risk Tolerance

Risk tolerance is not about courage. It is about responsibility. As the primary provider, my risk tolerance was conservative, and that is wisdom, not weakness. If you allocate $5,000 to trading, risking $1,000 per trade can be reckless.

Ask yourself:

- Would a 10% drawdown affect my household stability?
- Am I trading with discretionary income only?
- Can I emotionally handle consecutive losses?

Preservation comes before acceleration. A disciplined structure might look like this:

- Risk 1% per trade ($50 on a $5,000 account).
- Accept that losses are part of the process.
- Prioritize account survival over rapid growth.

4. Your Time Commitment

Time is often more limited than capital. If you only have one hour per day, your strategy must fit within that boundary. Overcommitting time creates stress. Stress leads to impulsive decisions. Sustainable trading respects your schedule. As a working mother, my day included corporate responsibilities, parenting, household management, and professional development. That meant my trading time was limited to 30–60 minutes in the morning and 30 minutes in the evening.

My structure included:

- Pre-set Alerts
- Daily 15-minute Chart Review
- Weekly Sunday Analysis

5. Your Review Process

Growth happens during review, not during the trade itself. With limited capital, every trade becomes a lesson. After each trade, record:

- Why you entered
- Why you exited
- Whether you followed your rules
- What emotions were present
- Weekly review questions might include:
- Did I follow my trading plan?
- Did I respect my risk limits?
- Did I trade out of discipline or boredom?
- What can I improve next week?

Monthly reflection:

- Is my strategy aligned with my goals?
- Is my risk appropriate for my current life stage?
- Am I improving consistency?
- Discipline compounds over time.

As mentioned earlier, use the Trading Success Logbookto track your trading activities systematically, which can provide valuable insights and help you improve your trading skills over time.

Robust Trading Strategy

A strategy should clearly outline markets traded, entry criteria, exit criteria, position sizing rules, and risk management parameters. Choose a strategy aligned with your time availability and emotional tolerance. Now we delve deeper into some strategies below:

1. Trend Following

Trend following assumes markets move in sustained directions. Traders identify established trends and participate in them.

Therefore, it is best suited for:

- Individuals who prefer patience

- Traders with limited screen time
- Directional market conditions

2. Mean Reversion

Mean reversion assumes a price will return to its average after becoming extended.

This strategy is best suited for:

- Range-bound markets
- Traders comfortable managing reversals
- Structured setups with defined risk

3. Breakout Trading

Breakout trading focuses on entering trades when the price moves beyond support or resistance levels.

Best suited for:

- Structured traders
- Those using alerts
- Individuals who cannot constantly monitor

4. Scalping

Scalping involves capturing small price movements rapidly. This strategy is generally less suitable for full-time professionals.

This technique requires:

- Continuous screen time
- Fast execution
- High concentration

For most beginners, trend following or breakout trading is easier to manage than scalping. Most sustainable for working professionals are trend following (short-term swing style) and Breakout Trading with price alerts. On the other hand, less suitable strategies are Scalping and High-frequency Trading for full-time professionals exercising Side Hustle Trading. Choose sustainability over excitement.

If you are starting out, the recommendations are:

- Trade one market only.
- Use one strategy.
- Risk no more than 1–2% per trade.
- Focus on consistency before profitability.
- Master one setup before expanding.

Risk Management Measures

Risk management protects capital and builds long-term viability. Entering Side Hustle Trading opens a meaningful opportunity. When you commit to structured risk practices, you cultivate stability and long-term perspective. Chapter 7of this book delves even deeper into risk management concepts.

Let's delve into the techniques and strategies advocated by experts in the field of Side Hustle Trading:

1. Position Sizing

One of the fundamental principles of risk management is position sizing. Traders should determine the size of each trade based on their risk tolerance, account size, and the probability of success. Traders determine the size of each trade based on factors such as risk tolerance, account size, and the probability of success (*Investopedia, n.d.*). By allocating a predetermined percentage of their capital to each trade, traders can limit potential losses and maintain consistency in their trading approach.

2. Setting Stop-Loss Orders

Stop-loss orders are essential tools for controlling risk in Side Hustle Trading. Setting stop-loss orders is a widely used risk management technique that allows traders to define the maximum amount they are willing to lose on a particular trade (*Investopedia, n.d.*). Stop-loss orders help traders exit losing positions promptly, preventing emotional decision-making and preserving capital during periods of market volatility.

3. Diversification

Diversification is another critical aspect of risk management. By spreading capital across different asset classes, sectors, or trading strategies, traders can reduce the impact of adverse market events on their overall portfolio (*Optionstrading.org, n.d.*). Diversification helps mitigate specific risks associated with individual assets or sectors while potentially capturing opportunities for growth in other areas of the market.

4. Risk-Reward Ratio Evaluation

Traders should aim for trades where the potential reward outweighs the risk involved. Traders assess the potential reward relative to the associated risk of each trade to identify favorable opportunities (*Investopedia, n.d.*). By adhering to favorable risk-reward ratios, traders can maintain a positive expectancy over time, even if not all trades are profitable.

Understanding the principles of risk management and implementing proven strategies like position sizing, setting stop-loss orders, diversification, and evaluating risk-reward ratios enable traders to confidently and systematically navigate market uncertainties.

Chapter Summary

In this chapter, we examined the essential elements of constructing a structured trading plan, including defining realistic financial goals, aligning strategy with lifestyle, respecting risk tolerance, managing time effectively, and implementing disciplined review processes. Side Hustle Trading is not about adrenaline. It is about structure, consistency, and responsibility. When aligned with your real-life responsibilities, trading becomes a disciplined tool for financial growth, not a gamble. From meticulous market analysis to strategic risk management, each aspect of the trading plan is dissected to provide readers with actionable insights for enhancing their trading performance. Furthermore, the chapter highlights the significance of discipline in adhering to trading plans, setting clear goals, and embracing consistent routines. By integrating these elements cohesively, individuals can fortify their position in the Side Hustle Trading arena, positioning themselves for long-term success and financial empowerment.

In the next chapter, we will explore self-management strategies in greater detail to deepen your emotional fortitude towards Futures Trading.

Chapter Three

Self-Management - Trading Psychology and Emotions

"The best way to measure your investing success is not by whether you're beating the market but by whether you've put in place a financial plan and a behavioral discipline that are likely to get you where you want to go." - Benjamin Graham

In the high-stakes world of trading, success is not solely determined by market analysis or technical expertise. It also hinges significantly on mastering the psychological aspects of trading and effectively managing one's emotions. Emotions such as fear, greed, and uncertainty can profoundly influence trading decisions and impact overall performance. Ultimately, the capacity to effectively manage emotions and uphold a balanced mindset distinguishes beginners from seasoned traders who flourish in the dynamic and competitive realm of finance.

Robust Self-Management Practices

To effectively navigate the complexities of trading and uphold sound financial decision-making, it is imperative to implement robust self-management practices. Let's delve into key techniques and principles aimed at bolstering self-management, ensuring informed decisions, and mitigating potential risks:

1. Educate Yourself

Before embarking on your trading journey, it is imperative to acquaint yourself with the fundamentals. For example, for cryptocurrency trading, a trader may deepen their knowledge of blockchain technology; the diverse array of cryptocurrencies and market trends empowers traders to navigate confidently. Dedicate time to understanding different coins, their underlying technologies, and prevailing market trends; doing so will furnish you with invaluable insights that shape your trading strategies.

2. Set Clear Goals and Limits

Define your financial goals and set profit-taking and stop-loss levels for each trade. Stick to these limits to prevent emotional decision-making and limit potential losses. Setting clear goals and limits is essential for maintaining discipline and managing risk in cryptocurrency trading. Define your financial objectives and establish profit-taking and stop-loss levels for each trade.

Adhering to predetermined limits helps prevent emotional decision-making and ensures that you exit trades according to your predefined parameters. By setting clear goals and limits, you maintain control over your trading activities and protect your capital from unnecessary losses.

3. Keep Emotions in Check

Guard against emotional decision-making, as it often triggers impulsive and irrational trading choices. Aim to retain emotional equilibrium and rely on research and analysis rather than succumbing to fear or greed. Emotional decision-making, fueled by fear or greed, tends to result in impulsive and irrational trading actions.

Foster a rational and analytical mindset, grounded in thorough research, technical analysis, and market trends, to guide your decisions. Cultivating emotional discipline enables you to make reasoned and strategic trading choices, enhancing your prospects for success in the cryptocurrency market.

4. Stay Updated on News and Market Trends

Stay informed about the latest news and developments in the cryptocurrency market. News can significantly impact prices, so being aware of current events can help you make better-informed trading decisions.

By remaining abreast of the latest news and developments, traders can better anticipate market reactions and make informed trading decisions. Keeping an eye on industry news, regulatory updates, and technological innovations enables traders to assess potential impacts on cryptocurrency prices and adjust their strategies accordingly.

Additionally, staying informed about market sentiment and emerging trends can provide valuable insights into investor behavior and market dynamics, helping traders stay ahead of the curve. This book also includes recommendations for finance news sites, among other valuable resources, to help you stay informed and make informed decisions about your trading activities.

5. Use Technical Analysis

Dive into technical analysis, a method that studies past price data and uses indicators to forecast future price movements. Becoming skilled in technical analysis can help you spot trends and make more accurate predictions. Before investing any of your own money, it's crucial to spend time learning how to read charts and understand technical indicators.

Allocate a specific timeframe for observation and learning without investing any capital. This period allows you to familiarize yourself with various technical analysis tools, such as moving averages, the relative strength index (RSI), and Fibonacci retracement levels.

By honing your skills in technical analysis, you can gain valuable insights into market trends, identify potential entry and exit points, and effectively manage risk in your trading endeavors. Remember, the knowledge gained through learning and observation lays the foundation for informed decision-making and successful trading strategies.

As you commence your journey in futures trading, bear in mind that this is only the starting point. Look forward to discovering further insights and strategies in the forthcoming chapters. We're committed to supporting you at each stage as you explore the exciting opportunities within futures trading.

Emotional Triggers in Real Life

1. Fear

Fear shows up when:

- You hesitate to enter a valid setup because you "can't afford to lose."

- You exit early because you feel anxious.
- You reduce position size impulsively after one loss.

In my case, fear was strongest during periods when household finances felt strained. If support payments were delayed, my tolerance for drawdown shrank dramatically. Fear is often amplified by external stress.

2. Greed

Greed does not always look like arrogance. Sometimes it looks like desperation.

- Increasing position size after a win to "recover faster."
- Taking trades outside your plan to "make up for a bad week."
- Holding a profitable trade too long because you need the money.

When finances feel uncertain, greed disguises itself as urgency.

3. Overcontrol

When life feels unpredictable, trading can become an attempt to regain control. This often leads to:

- Overanalyzing charts

- Trading too frequently
- Forcing trades during low-quality setups

Markets cannot be controlled. Only risk can.

Practical Scenarios with Step-by-Step Responses

Below are real-world emotional situations and structured responses.

Scenario 1: A Losing Trade During Financial Stress

You take a trade, and it hits your stop-loss. That same week, a support payment did not arrive.

Emotion:

- Anxiety
- Frustration
- Tight chest
- Urge to "make it back."

Pause immediately. Do not enter another trade. Step away from the screen for 10–15 minutes.

Ask:

- Did I follow my plan?

- Was the risk within limits?

If the answer to any of these questions is "yes," the loss is statistical, not personal.

Secondly, write in your journal: "Loss within rules. Emotional reaction triggered by external stress." Reduce size on the next trade if needed, but do not revenge trade. You protect capital by protecting your emotional state first.

Scenario 2: A Winning Streak Creates Overconfidence

You win three trades in a row. You are on a winning streak! You may think internally, "I understand this market now." Therefore, there is a temptation to double the position size.

Emotion:

- Confidence shifts toward invincibility.

Once again, pause and evaluate. The recommendation would be not to increase the size until the next review period (weekly or monthly). Re-read your written risk rules.

Ask:

- Has my strategy changed?
- Or has luck simply aligned?

After delay and reviewing the strategy, the decision may be to maintain the original position size. Overconfidence destroys consistency faster than fear.

Scenario 3: Fatigue After a Long Workday

You had a demanding day at work. Parenting or household responsibilities followed. You feel mentally drained. But there is a temptation to enter a trade out of boredom or distraction.

Emotion:

- Irritability
- Reduced focus.

Yes, you got it; pause and ask, "Would I take this trade if I were mentally clear?" If the answer is uncertain, the recommendation would be not to trade. Instead, replace trading time with review only, no live positions. Close charts early. Protect mental energy. A missed trade is better than a forced one.

Scenario 4: Financial Urgency

Unexpected expense. Legal fees. Household repair. Financial pressure increases. The temptation may be to take larger trades to "solve" the problem.

Emotion: Urgency

In this scenario, you should acknowledge that trading is not an emergency fund. Recommit to the 1–2% risk rule. Reduce trading frequency if emotional tension is high. Separate trading capital mentally from household expenses. Trading should never become a survival mechanism.

You need to practice discipline under pressure. When a financial partnership was unequal and support unreliable, something important to remember is that trading could not become another unstable variable. That shift is powerful. Self-management becomes about protecting stability, not chasing opportunity. We cannot control another adult's follow-through. But we can control position size, stop-loss placement, daily loss limits, whether to trade at all.

Structured Self-Management Practices

Below are some suggestions of mindset and checklists that can be utilized during trading. As mentioned earlier, we highly recommend journaling at Trading Success Logbook.

1. Pre-Trade Checklist

Before every trade:

- Is this setup within my plan?
- Is the risk within my predefined percentage?

- Am I emotionally neutral?

If any answer is no, do not trade. Plan for a daily max loss limit. For example, if two trades hit stop-loss, stop trading for the day. This prevents emotional spirals.

2. Weekly Emotional Audit

Awareness builds discipline. Every week, ask:

- Did external stress influence my trading?
- Did I trade out of fear or urgency?
- Did I respect my rules even when uncomfortable?

3. Education as Emotional Stability

Knowledge reduces fear. Education holds utmost importance. Grasping market trends, interpreting technical analysis, and staying abreast of industry advancements equip you to make informed decisions and confidently navigate market fluctuations. Through portfolio diversification, realistic goal-setting, and emotional balance, you position yourself to seize opportunities and withstand market volatility with resilience.

Education turns uncertainty into structured probability. Before risking meaningful capital, invest time in:

- Understanding contracts
- Studying volatility patterns
- Learning technical analysis
- Observing markets without trading

4. Financial Self-Protection

When you are a full-time professional and primary provider, trading must serve your life, not destabilize it. Self-management in trading is not just about improving performance. It is about protecting:

- Your capital
- Your confidence
- Your mental health
- Your household stability

5. The Role of Self-Care

Mental resilience outside the markets strengthens resilience inside them. If you are carrying many responsibilities, stress accumulates. Self-care is not indulgence; it is maintenance.

When life feels grounded, trading decisions stabilize. For me, that included:

- Early morning quiet time
- Exercise
- Skill development at work
- Creative outlets
- Time with my child without screens

Chapter Summary

In this chapter, we delved into the critical role of emotional intelligence and discipline in the world of trading. The chapter emphasizes the profound impact of emotions such as fear, greed, and uncertainty on trading decisions and overall performance. Through insightful analysis and practical strategies, readers gain valuable insights into managing emotions effectively to achieve long-term success in trading.

We explored the emotional realities behind trading, practical step-by-step responses to emotional triggers, the importance of discipline and self-care, and structured self-management systems.

Trading psychology is not theoretical. It is lived. By acknowledging the innate human tendency to respond emotionally to market fluctuations, traders are empowered to cultivate resilience through mindfulness practices, cognitive reframing, and maintaining a balanced perspective.

By integrating self-management practices into their trading approach, individuals can mitigate the influence of emotions, uphold rational decision-making, and ultimately enhance their prospects for success in the dynamic world of finance. By acknowledging your real-life responsibilities and building emotional safeguards into your trading plan, you position yourself for sustainable growth.

In the next chapter, we will continue building a structure around execution and performance refinement and the specifics of Future Trading.

Chapter Four

Basics of Futures Trading

"I make no attempt to forecast the market, my efforts are devoted to finding undervalued securities." - Warren Buffett

Trading Futures is not as popular as options or trading regular stocks. In previous chapters, we delved into the basics and psychology of trading applicable to any general trading. But in this chapter, we are delving into Futures Trading, which will be the main focus from here on. Futures trading entails individuals forecasting future price changes for commodities, financial instruments, stock indexes, interest rates, and currencies in organized financial markets.

Various strategies are employed in futures markets, including trend following, spread trading, arbitrage, and hedging. While futures offer substantial opportunities, they also carry inherent risks due to leverage and price volatility. Success requires discipline, structured risk management, and a thorough understanding of contract mechanics. This chapter will provide readers with their first glimpse of a detailed introduction to futures.

Definition of Futures Trading

Futures trading involves the buying and selling of standardized contracts, known as futures contracts, that obligate the two parties to agree to buy or sell the underlying asset at a predetermined price and date in the future (*Investopedia, n.d.*). At its core, futures trading involves the buying and selling of standardized contracts, known as futures contracts.

These contracts are standardized in terms of quantity, quality (where applicable), expiration month, and settlement procedures, which promotes transparency, fairness, and liquidity. These contracts are traded on organized exchanges, such as the Chicago Mercantile Exchange (CME) and the Intercontinental Exchange (ICE), which provide a centralized marketplace for buyers and sellers to execute trades (*Schwab, n.d.*).

Unlike options contracts, which grant the buyer the right but not the obligation to transact, futures contracts create a binding obligation for both parties. At expiration, the contract must be settled either through physical delivery (common in certain commodity markets) or cash settlement (common in stock index futures).

However, most retail traders close their positions before expiration and do not take delivery. These contracts are not limited to traditional commodities such as wheat or crude oil. The contracts also cover a broad range of asset classes.

For example, futures contracts may encompass the following:

- Agricultural Commodities (corn, wheat, soybeans)
- Energy Products (crude oil, natural gas)
- Precious Metals (gold, silver)
- Stock Indexes (S&P 500, Nasdaq)
- Interest Rates
- Currencies

This wide coverage allows participants to hedge risk, speculate on price movement, or diversify portfolios.

Purpose of Futures Trading

The purpose of futures trading extends beyond mere speculation. Participants in futures markets, including hedgers and speculators, use futures contracts to hedge against adverse price movements or to profit from anticipated price changes (*Investopedia, n.d.*). Hedgers, such as farmers and manufacturers, use futures contracts to lock in prices for their products or commodities, thereby reducing exposure to price volatility (*CME Group, n.d.*).

Speculators, on the other hand, seek to profit from price movements by buying or selling futures contracts without the intention of taking physical delivery of the underlying asset (*TD Ameritrade, n.d.*). Hedgers, such as farmers, manufacturers, airlines, and financial institutions, use futures contracts to lock in prices and reduce exposure to unfavorable price changes.

By locking in future prices through hedging strategies, these participants can safeguard against potential losses resulting from unfavorable market movements. On the other hand, speculators capitalize on price differentials and market trends to generate profits by taking positions in futures contracts without the intention of physical delivery. This interplay between hedgers and speculators fosters liquidity and price efficiency in futures markets, contributing to overall market stability.

For example, an airline may purchase crude oil futures to hedge against rising fuel costs. Speculators, including individual traders and institutional investors, seek to profit from anticipated price movements.

They provide liquidity to the market, making it easier for hedgers to enter and exit positions efficiently. The interaction between hedgers and speculators supports efficient price discovery and market stability.

Mechanics of Futures Trading

The mechanics of futures trading revolve around standardized contracts, exchange platforms, and intermediary brokerage services that facilitate trade execution. To initiate a futures trade, traders must open a brokerage account with a firm that is approved to trade futures (*E-Futures, n.d.*).

They can then place orders to buy or sell futures contracts through the brokerage platform, which matches buyers with sellers in the futures market (*RJO Futures, n.d.*). Futures contracts typically specify the quantity, quality, delivery date, and price of the underlying asset, providing clarity and transparency for market participants.

They are standardized agreements that specify:

- Contract size
- Tick size (minimum price movement)
- Tick value (dollar value per tick)
- Expiration month
- Settlement method

Traders can access futures markets through regulated exchanges such as the Chicago Mercantile Exchange (CME) or electronic trading platforms offered by brokerage firms. By opening futures trading accounts and adhering to margin requirements, traders can execute buy or sell orders, initiate positions, and manage their portfolios with ease.

This seamless integration of technology and financial infrastructure has democratized access to futures trading, enabling individuals and institutions alike to participate in global markets and capitalize on price movements. When researching a platform to trade in, traders may explore options like Charles Schwab, Fidelity, Interactive Brokers, TD Ameritrade, and E*TRADE, among others, which offer futures trading services.

These platforms provide user-friendly interfaces, comprehensive research tools, and robust customer support to assist traders in their investment endeavors (*Investopedia, n.d.*).

There are two key margin requirements:

- Initial Margin – Required to open a position.
- Maintenance Margin – Minimum balance required to maintain the position.

If the account balance falls below the maintenance margin due to losses, a margin call is issued. Leverage allows traders to control large notional values with relatively small capital deposits. While this enhances capital efficiency, it also magnifies both profits and losses.

Traders must also remain cognizant of the fees associated with participating in futures trading. These fees encompass commissions, margin interest rates, and exchange fees, all of which can influence overall profitability.

Moreover, traders need to recognize that any profits derived from futures trading are subject to taxation under the tax laws of their jurisdiction. Hence, seeking guidance from tax professionals is highly recommended to ensure compliance with regulations and enhance tax efficiency in futures trading endeavors.

Key Participants in Futures Trading

Futures markets are comprised of various participants, including hedgers, speculators, and market makers. Hedgers are producers or consumers of the underlying asset who use futures contracts to protect against adverse price movements.

Speculators, including individual traders and institutional investors, seek to profit from price fluctuations by taking positions in futures contracts based on their market outlook. Market makers, often brokerage firms or financial institutions, facilitate liquidity in the futures market by providing continuous buy and sell quotes for futures contracts (*Udemy, n.d.*).

Essentially, built on standardized contracts, deliberate strategies, and effective market mechanisms, futures trading enables traders to manage volatility, mitigate uncertainty, and pursue financial goals with confidence. As technology advances and markets become increasingly interconnected, futures trading remains a fundamental aspect of portfolio diversification and strategic investment planning worldwide.

In conclusion, Futures markets consist of several key participants:

- Hedgers: Reduce price risk.
- Speculators: Seek profit from price movement.
- Arbitrageurs: Exploit pricing inefficiencies.
- Market makers: Provide liquidity by continuously quoting prices.
- Clearinghouses guarantee performance of contracts, significantly reducing counterparty default risk.

Numerical Example: A Complete Futures Trade

Let us walk through a full example using the E-mini S&P 500 futures contract (ES).

You deposit $15,000 into your futures account and buy 1 ES contract at 5,000. Assume:

- S&P 500 Index = 5,000
- Contract Multiplier = $50 per point
- Notional Value = 5,000 × $50 = $250,000

- Initial Margin Requirement = $12,000 (example value)

Scenario 1: Market Moves in Your Favor

The index rises to 5,010.

Price movement = 10 points

Dollar value per point = $50

Profit = 10 × $50 = $500

Your account balance increases to $15,500 (before commissions).

Scenario 2: Market Moves Against You

The index falls to 4,980.

Price movement = -20 points

Loss = 20 × $50 = $1,000

Your account balance decreases to $14,000.

If losses continue and your balance falls below the maintenance margin requirement, you must deposit additional funds to maintain the position.

When you close the position at 5,015:

15 points × $50 = $750 profit

The trade is complete, and the gain is realized.

This example demonstrates how relatively small index movements can result in meaningful financial impact due to leverage.

Understanding Futures Contracts

As explained earlier, Futures contracts are defined by their standardized attributes, detailing the quantity, quality, transaction price, and settlement date of the underlying asset. This standardization promotes transparency and liquidity in futures markets, facilitating seamless entry and exit for investors. For instance, a futures contract for gold may specify the delivery of 100 troy ounces at $1,800 per ounce on a predetermined future date. One of the fundamental characteristics of futures contracts is their obligation to buy or sell the underlying asset at a future date, regardless of market conditions (*Bajaj Finserv, 2022*). This aspect distinguishes futures contracts from other derivative instruments, such as options, in which the holder has the right but not the obligation to execute the contract (*Angel One, 2022*).

Futures contracts serve multiple purposes in financial markets, including price discovery, risk management, and speculation (*Investopedia, 2022*). For instance, producers and consumers often use futures contracts to hedge against adverse price movements, thereby mitigating the risk of financial losses arising from market volatility (*Britannica, 2022*). Futures contracts promote transparency through standardization. Every contract clearly defines quantity of the asset, delivery terms, expiration date, price increments to the minimum.

This structure allows efficient entry and exit. It also enables price discovery, reflecting collective expectations of market participants. Airlines hedge fuel costs. Portfolio managers hedge stock exposure using index futures. Currency futures allow multinational firms to manage exchange rate risk. Moreover, futures contracts facilitate efficient price discovery by reflecting the collective expectations and sentiments of market participants regarding future asset prices (*CMC Group, 2022*). Investors can capitalize on price differentials and arbitrage opportunities across different futures contracts to generate profits (*India Infoline, 2022*).

However, it is essential to recognize the risks associated with futures trading, including the potential for substantial losses due to adverse price movements (*India Infoline, 2022*). Therefore, investors should conduct thorough research, assess their risk tolerance, and implement sound risk management strategies when engaging in futures trading (*5paisa, 2022*). Risk management is covered in more detail in the upcoming chapters.

As investors delve into futures trading, they will encounter both challenges and opportunities that require resilience, adaptability, and continuous learning. However, armed with a comprehensive understanding of futures contracts and their significance in the broader financial landscape, investors are better prepared to navigate market dynamics and seize emerging opportunities.

Micro-Futures vs Standard Futures (MES vs ES)

The CME introduced Micro E-mini futures to make futures trading more accessible. Micro futures are often more suitable for beginners, traders with smaller accounts, or those seeking finer control over position sizing. They allow traders to gain experience with reduced exposure.

Standard E-mini S&P 500 (ES)

Multiplier: $50 per point

Notional Value at 5,000: $250,000

Higher margin requirement

Larger P&L swings

Micro E-mini S&P 500 (MES)

Multiplier: $5 per point

Notional Value at 5,000: $25,000

Lower margin requirement

Smaller P&L swings

The MES contract is one-tenth the size of the ES contract.

For example:

If the market moves 10 points:

ES profit = 10 × $50 = $500

MES profit = 10 × $5 = $50

ES VS MES		
Feature	**ES (E-mini S&P 500)**	**MES (Micro E-mini S&P 500)**
Contract Size	$50 × S&P 500 Index	$5 × S&P 500 Index (1/10th of ES)
Use Case	Income generation, hedging, active trading	Learning, testing strategies, low-risk trading
Tick Value	$12.50 per tick	$1.25 per tick
Tick Size	0.25 index points	0.25 index points
Margin Requirement	Higher (varies by broker; often $10,000–$12,000+)	Much lower (often $1,000–$1,500)
Volatility Impact	Larger swings → larger P/L	Smaller swings → more controlled P/L
Best For	Experienced traders with larger accounts	Beginners, side-hustle traders, small accounts
Risk Level	Higher	Lower
Scalability	Good for large position sizing	Excellent for gradual scaling and practice
Liquidity	Extremely high	Very high (slightly lower than ES)

Figure 4.1: ES vs MES

Common Beginner Mistakes in Futures

Avoiding these common errors dramatically improves long-term survival.

- **Over-leveraging:** Trading the maximum number of contracts allowed by margin rather than appropriate position sizing.

- **Ignoring Tick Value:** Not fully understanding how much each price movement represents in dollar terms.

- **Trading Without Stop-Loss:** Hoping the market will reverse instead of defining risk in advance.
- **Revenge Trading:** Increasing size after a loss to "make it back."
- **Misunderstanding Margin:** Believing margin is the total cost rather than collateral.
- **Trading During High Volatility Without Experience:** Major news events can produce rapid price swings.
- **Failing to Review Trades:** Not journaling or analyzing mistakes.

Strategies for Trading Futures with Low Risk

Trading futures can be an exciting yet risky endeavor. It offers immense potential for profits, but the volatility of futures markets can also lead to substantial losses if not approached with caution. However, with the right strategies, traders can mitigate risks and increase their chances of success.

In this comprehensive guide, we explore various strategies for trading futures with low risk, allowing traders to navigate the markets with confidence:

1. Diversification

One key strategy for trading futures with low risk is diversifying the portfolio across different asset classes and instruments. Diversification involves allocating investments across multiple futures contracts or underlying assets, thereby minimizing the overall risk exposure to any particular market or sector (*Motilal Oswal, 2022*).

Diversification is a fundamental principle of risk management. Instead of concentrating all capital in a single asset or market, traders diversify their portfolios across different assets, sectors, and markets. Diversification helps reduce overall portfolio risk by spreading exposure across multiple investments with uncorrelated price movements. It allows traders to mitigate the impact of adverse events in any single market or asset class.

2. Trend Following

Another low-risk method for trading futures is trend-following. By identifying and trading with established trends, traders can capitalize on momentum while minimizing exposure to countertrend movements. Trend following is a popular strategy among futures traders. It involves identifying and following the prevailing market trends.

Traders look for assets with clear and sustained price movements in a particular direction and enter positions in line with the trend. By trading with the trend, traders aim to capitalize on momentum while minimizing exposure to countertrend reversals. Trading in the direction of established trends can reduce exposure to counter-trend reversals. Trend alignment increases probability, though it does not guarantee success.

3. Conservative Position Sizing

Proper position sizing is critical for managing risk in futures trading. Traders should determine the appropriate position size based on their account size, risk tolerance, and trading strategy. By limiting the size of each position relative to account equity, traders can control potential losses and avoid excessive risk exposure.

In addition to position sizing, setting stop-loss orders and regular portfolio rebalancing, adopting a conservative approach to position sizing helps protect capital during periods of market volatility.

4. Avoiding Over-Leverage

Over-leveraging is one of the fastest paths to account depletion. Over-leveraging is a common mistake among traders, particularly in futures markets, where leverage allows traders to control a large position with a relatively small amount of capital. Just because the margin allows multiple contracts does not mean you should trade them.

Be aware of the perils of over-leveraging in Futures Trading, and avoid excessive leverage that could amplify losses (*Small Exchange, n.d.*). While leverage can amplify returns, it also magnifies potential losses. Traders should be conservative in their use of leverage, ensuring that their positions are appropriately sized relative to their account equity and risk tolerance. Therefore, avoiding over-leverage is crucial for managing risk in futures trading. By limiting leverage, traders can reduce the impact of adverse price movements and protect their capital from excessive risk exposure.

5. Utilizing Technical Analysis

Technical analysis involves analyzing past price movements and market data to forecast future price trends. It helps traders identify key support and resistance levels, trend reversals, and other patterns that can inform trading decisions. By analyzing price charts and using technical indicators, traders can identify potential entry and exit points with favorable risk-reward ratios.

Use technical analysis to identify low-risk setups and to wait for confirmation signals before entering trades (*Daniel's Trading*, 2022). In futures trading, technical analysis can be a valuable tool for identifying entry and exit points, managing risk, and optimizing trading strategies. By studying price charts, indicators, and chart patterns, traders can gain insights into market dynamics and make more informed trading decisions. Technical analysis is covered more in details in Chapter 5.

Chapter Summary

The chapter intricately explores the operational mechanics of futures trading, shedding light on margin requirements, leverage, and the daily mark-to-market process. Traders are guided by the art of market analysis, where supply-and-demand fundamentals, technical indicators, and market sentiment converge to shape effective trading strategies. Amidst the allure of profit potential, the chapter underscores the significance of disciplined risk management practices.

Price volatility, leverage, and counterparty risks loom large, prompting traders to set clear objectives, implement stop-loss orders, diversify portfolios, and judiciously allocate capital to each trade. By integrating robust risk management techniques, traders forge a path of resilience and confidence in the dynamic landscape of futures markets, optimizing opportunities while fortifying against potential losses.

In the next chapter, we will explore the mechanics of futures markets in greater detail to deepen your technical understanding and improve execution precision.

Chapter Five

Technical Analysis for Futures Trading and Chart Patterns

"Thousands of experts study overbought indicators, head-and-shoulder patterns, put-call ratios, the Fed's policy on money supply...and they can't predict markets with any useful consistency, any more than the gizzard squeezers could tell the Roman emperors when the Huns would attack." - Peter Lynch

In futures markets, where leverage amplifies both opportunity and risk, understanding price structure is essential. At the heart of technical analysis are chart patterns, which serve as visual representations of market dynamics and investor sentiment. This chapter focuses on the foundations of technical analysis, the interpretation of chart patterns, and how these tools are applied practically in futures trading.

The Foundation of Technical Analysis

Technical analysis empowers traders to delve deeper into market dynamics and unearth potential profit opportunities. Through technical analysis, traders unravel chart patterns, pinpoint critical support and resistance levels, and decode various technical indicators to make well-informed decisions regarding trade entry and exit points.

Chart patterns encapsulate the collective actions of market participants, reflecting their perceptions, emotions, and expectations. Because markets are driven by fear, greed, momentum, and hesitation, price charts often form recognizable structures. These structures are called chart patterns, they reflect the battle between buyers and sellers.

Rather than predicting the future with certainty, technical analysis helps traders define probability and structure trades around measurable risk. By understanding the language of chart patterns and interpreting their implications, traders can make informed decisions and capitalize on emerging opportunities in the futures market.

Technical Analysis relies on three key assumptions:

- Market prices discount all known information.
- Price moves in trends.
- Human behavior and crowd psychology repeat over

time.

Understanding Chart Patterns

As described earlier, chart patterns encapsulate distinctive market expectations. They represent the psychology of market participants. For example, a head and shoulders pattern often heralds a discernible reversal in trend direction, whereas a triangle pattern portends an impending breakout. A trendline reflects sustained conviction:

- Support reflects defensive buying.
- Resistance reflects persistent selling.
- Reversal patterns reflect exhaustion.

Mastery in decoding these patterns empowers traders to accurately anticipate market movements and strategically position themselves to capitalize on prospective profits. Some common chart patterns include:

1. Trend Lines

Trend lines are diagonal lines drawn along swing highs or swing lows to define direction (Reference: Uptrend and Downtrend images). They help traders identify the overall trend and potential reversal points.

An **uptrend** forms when the price creates higher highs and higher lows. A rising trendline connects the higher lows and acts as dynamic support.

A **downtrend** forms when the price creates lower highs and lower lows. A descending trendline connects the lower highs and acts as dynamic resistance.

Trend lines serve three main purposes:

- Define directional bias
- Identify pullback opportunities
- Signal potential reversals when broken.

Figure 5.1: Uptrend Trendline Formation

Figure 5.2: Downtrend Trendline Formation

When a well-established trendline breaks with momentum, it often signals a structural shift in market control. However, trendlines are not precise price levels. They represent zones of interest rather than exact turning points.

2. Support and Resistance Levels

Support and resistance levels represent key thresholds at which significant buying or selling activity is anticipated to materialize (Reference: Support and Resistance images). Support and resistance are horizontal levels where price historically struggled to move beyond. Rather than guessing direction, traders observe how the price behaves at these levels.

Support forms when buying pressure repeatedly prevents the price from falling further.

Resistance forms when selling pressure repeatedly prevents the price from rising higher.

These levels carry psychological significance because traders remember previous reactions and have the potential to shape subsequent price dynamics. When prices revisit these areas, order flow often increases again. Support can become resistance after a breakdown. Resistance can become support after a breakout. In futures trading, these levels help define Entry Zones, Stop Placement, Profit Targets, Breakout Confirmation.

Figure 5.3: Support level

Figure 5.4: Resistance level

3. Head and Shoulders Pattern

The head and shoulders pattern is a classic reversal formation (Reference: Head and Shoulders image). The head and shoulders pattern is a distinct reversal formation identifiable by three peaks, with the central peak (the head) positioned higher than the surrounding two (the shoulders). This pattern typically indicates a potential shift in the prevailing trend, transitioning either from bullish to bearish or vice versa.

It consists of:

- A left shoulder
- A higher peak (the head)
- A lower peak (the right shoulder)
- A neckline connecting the reaction lows

This pattern represents weakening momentum. Buyers push the price higher to form the head, but the subsequent rally fails to exceed that high. When the price breaks below the neckline, it confirms that sellers have gained control. The inverse head and shoulders signals the opposite: a potential bullish reversal after a downtrend. The pattern becomes meaningful only after neckline confirmation. Anticipating prematurely increases risk.

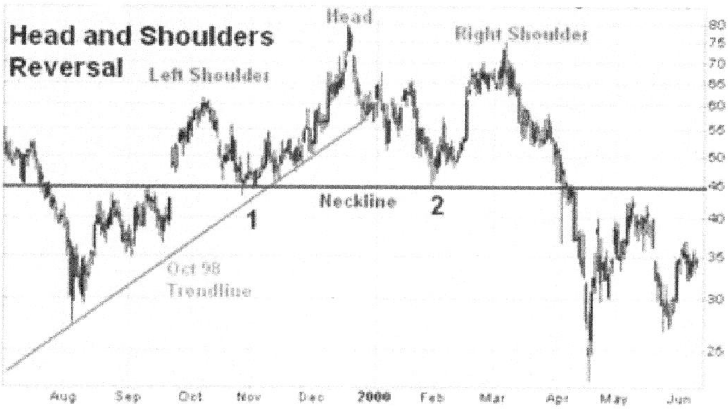

Figure 5.5: Head and shoulders reversal pattern

4. Double Tops and Double Bottoms

Double tops and double bottoms are reversal patterns that reflect failed continuation attempts (Reference: Double Top and Double Bottom images). Double tops and bottoms represent reversal patterns observed when the price reaches a comparable high (double top) or low (double bottom) twice before undergoing a reversal in direction. These patterns signify the potential exhaustion of either buying or selling pressure in the market.

A **double top** forms when the price reaches a high, pulls back, retests the high, and fails to break through. This indicates weakening buying pressure. Double tops resemble an "M" shape. A **double bottom** forms when the price reaches a low, rebounds, revisits the low, and holds. This signals seller exhaustion.

Double bottoms resemble a "W" shape. The key level in both formations is the "neckline" or breakout level between the two peaks or troughs. Confirmation occurs when the price breaks through that level. These formations are particularly useful in futures markets where momentum exhaustion often leads to sharp reversals.

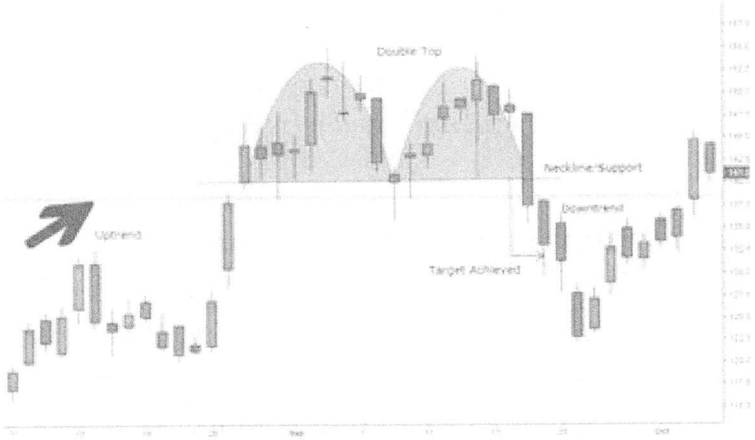

Figure 5.6: Double top reversal pattern (M shape)

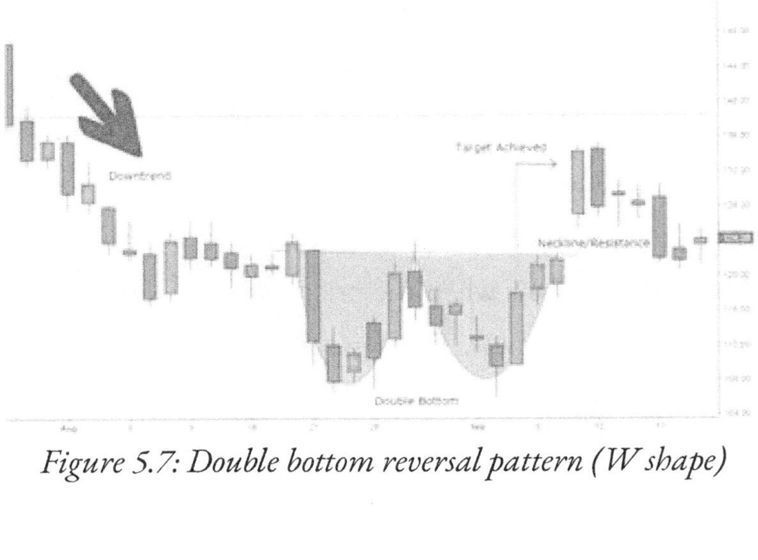

Figure 5.7: Double bottom reversal pattern (W shape)

Key Technical Indicators

Chart patterns provide structural insight. Indicators provide momentum and confirmation. Indicators should confirm structure, not replace it. These indicators, including moving averages, relative strength index (RSI), stochastic oscillator, and MACD (Moving Average Convergence Divergence), offer quantitative insights into market momentum, volatility, and trend strength.

By analyzing these indicators, traders can assess underlying market sentiment and pinpoint potential entry or exit points for trades. Combining chart patterns with technical indicators allows traders to develop a holistic understanding of market dynamics and make well-informed trading decisions. The key indicators are described in details below.

1. Moving Averages

Moving averages smooth price data and help define trend direction for traders to make holistic decisions. They are most effective when used alongside a price structure.

A rising moving average confirms upward bias.

A falling moving average confirms downward bias.

Crossovers between short-term and long-term moving averages can signal trend shifts, but they are lagging tools.

2. Relative Strength Index (RSI)

Traders use Technical Analysis to identify low-risk opportunities. RSI measures momentum and overbought/oversold conditions.

Above 70: potential overbought condition

Below 30: potential oversold condition

RSI is most powerful when divergence appears. If price makes a new high but RSI does not, momentum may be weakening. Divergence does not guarantee reversal, but it increases awareness of potential exhaustion.

3. MACD (Moving Average Convergence Divergence)

MACD measures the relationship between two moving averages. Traders look for Crossovers and Divergence. Through momentum expansion or contraction, MACD is useful for confirming trend strength rather than predicting turning points.

4. Bollinger Bands

Bollinger Bands expand and contract based on volatility. When a price moves outside the bands, it may signal strong continuation or potential exhaustion. Volatility compression often precedes breakout expansion.

5. Combine Indicators With Structure

Successful traders always start with market structure first, then use indicators only to confirm what price is already showing. Use this simple flow of identifying trend direction, mark support and resistance, wait for a pullback or breakout, use indicators (RSI, MACD, MAs, Volume) to confirm the setup, enter only when the structure + indicator agree.

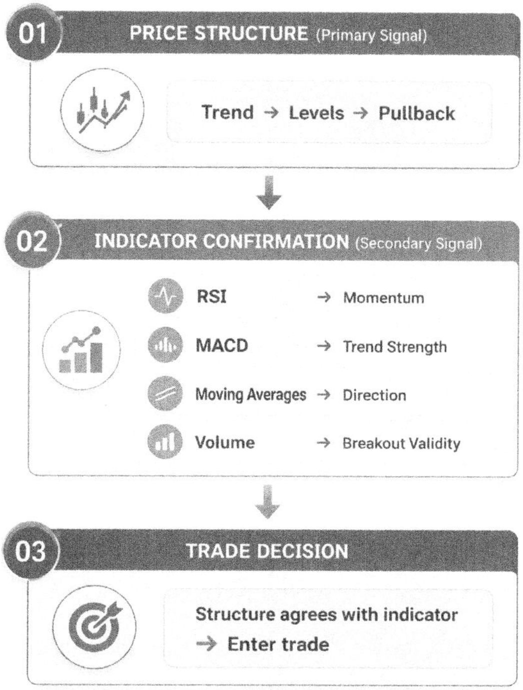

Figure 5.8: Combine Indicators With Structure

Understanding Candlestick Charts

Candlestick charts are powerful tools in technical analysis, providing traders with valuable insights into price movements and market sentiment. Derived from Japanese rice merchants in the 1700s, these charts have evolved into a standard feature in modern trading platforms. In this guide, we'll delve into the intricacies of candlestick charts, elucidating their components and how to interpret them effectively.

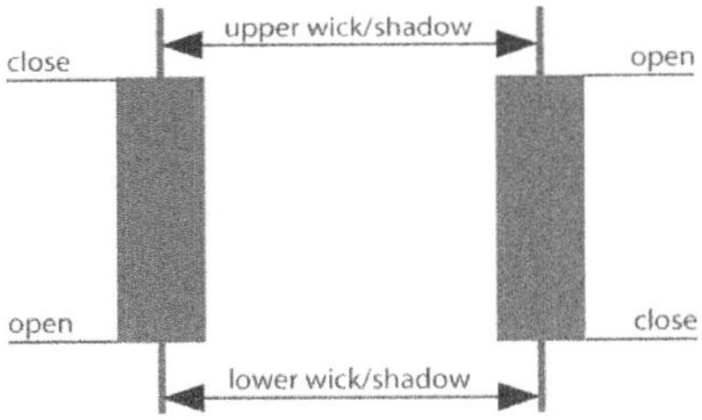

Figure 5.9: Candlestick chart overview

1. Basic Structure:

Candlestick charts consist of individual "candlesticks," each representing a specific time frame, such as minutes, hours, days, or weeks. Each candlestick comprises a "body" and "wicks" or "shadows" at both ends. The body illustrates the opening and closing prices, while the wicks indicate the high and low prices during the given time frame (*DailyFX, n.d.*).

2. Bullish and Bearish Candlesticks:

- **Bullish Candlestick:** A bullish candlestick forms when the closing price is higher than the opening price. It typically appears green or white and signifies bullish momentum (*DailyFX, n.d.*).

- **Bearish Candlestick:** Conversely, a bearish candlestick occurs when the closing price is lower than the opening price, denoted by a red or black body. It reflects bearish sentiment in the market (*DailyFX, n.d.*).

3. Candlestick Patterns:

Candlestick patterns are formations created by multiple candlesticks in succession, offering insights into potential market reversals or continuations (*DailyFX, n.d.*). Some common patterns include:

- **Doji:** Signifying indecision, a Doji forms when the opening and closing prices are virtually equal, resulting in a small-bodied candlestick (*DailyFX, n.d.*).

- **Hammer and Hanging Man:** These patterns consist of

small bodies and long lower wicks, indicating potential bullish reversals (hammer) or bearish reversals (hanging man) (*DailyFX, n.d.*).

- **Engulfing Patterns:** Bullish engulfing patterns occur when a bullish candlestick "engulfs" the previous bearish candlestick, suggesting a shift towards bullish sentiment, and vice versa for bearish engulfing patterns (*DailyFX, n.d.*).

4. Interpreting Candlestick Charts:

Long bullish candlesticks with minimal wicks indicate strong bullish momentum, while long bearish candlesticks suggest significant selling pressure. Patterns such as hammers and shooting stars at key support or resistance levels can signal potential trend reversals. Confirmation from other technical indicators enhances the reliability of candlestick patterns (*DailyFX, n.d.*).

Understanding candlestick charts empowers traders to make informed decisions based on market dynamics and sentiment. By incorporating candlestick analysis into their trading strategies, traders gain a deeper understanding of price action and improve their ability to identify lucrative trading opportunities.

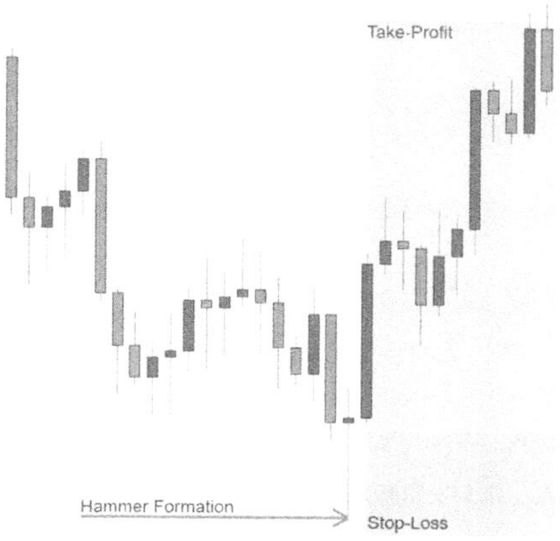

Figure 5.10: Bullish and bearish candlestick momentum

Applying Technical Analysis to Futures Trading

Venturing into futures trading introduces traders to a dynamic landscape filled with opportunities and challenges. It involves the study of historical price data, chart patterns, and technical indicators to forecast future price action and identify trading opportunities (*LinkedIn, 2022*).

Technical analysis operates on the premise that historical price movements repeat themselves, allowing traders to anticipate future trends and make informed trading decisions (*City Index, n. d.*). Most importantly, technical analysis becomes powerful when it defines risk clearly. Low-risk setups share three characteristics:

- Clear structural level (support, resistance, trendline)
- Confirming pattern (double bottom, breakout, reversal)

- Defined invalidation point (logical stop level)

For example: Price forms a double bottom at major support, RSI shows bullish divergence, and a breakout occurs above the neckline. The stop can be placed below the second low. Risk is defined before entry. Low risk does not mean high-probability certainty.

It means the risk-to-reward structure is favorable. A head-and-shoulders pattern forming against strong macro fundamentals may fail. A breakout during major economic releases may experience excessive slippage. Traders can further integrate technical analysis with a broader strategy. Structure plus context improves outcomes. Technical analysis must operate within:

- Risk management rules
- Defined position sizing
- Psychological discipline
- Awareness of macro context
- Continuous Adaptation

Markets evolve, volatility regimes change, and correlations shift. Technical analysis is a skill developed through observation and repetition, not memorization. Traders must continually:

- Refine pattern recognition,

- Review failed setups,
- Adjust to volatility expansion and contraction,
- Avoid overreliance on any single indicator.

Most trading platforms come with technical analysis. Depending on what platform you choose, you can make confident information trading decisions. I have used the TradingView (www.tradingview.com) platform to periodically review technical analysis, where I created a personalized watchlist. Trading platforms are discussed in details in Chapter 9.

Chapter Summary

Technical analysis provides a structured method for interpreting price behavior in futures markets. Through trend lines, support and resistance, head and shoulders formations, and double tops and bottoms, traders gain insight into market psychology and directional probability. Indicators such as moving averages, RSI, MACD, and Bollinger Bands supplement structural analysis by measuring momentum and volatility.

When combined thoughtfully and applied within disciplined risk management, technical analysis enables traders to identify structured opportunities with defined risk parameters. It is not a prediction tool. It is a probability framework. Mastery lies not in recognizing patterns alone but in executing them with patience, discipline, and clarity.

Technical analysis forms the bedrock of futures trading, empowering traders to decipher market trends and forecast price movements. This segment delves deep into the nuanced principles of technical analysis, equipping traders with indispensable tools to interpret chart patterns and technical indicators effectively.

From understanding trend lines and support/resistance levels to recognizing intricate patterns like head and shoulders, traders glean insights into the collective behaviors of market participants, enabling them to make informed decisions and capitalize on emerging opportunities.

As traders venture into the futures market, embracing technical analysis becomes imperative, providing a systematic approach to navigate market fluctuations and achieve trading success within the dynamic realm of the financial landscape.

Chapter Six

Fundamental Analysis for Futures Trading

"The stock market is a device to transfer money from the impatient to the patient." - Warren Buffett

In futures markets, price is ultimately driven by supply, demand, macroeconomic conditions, and expectations of future events. Fundamental analysis seeks to understand those drivers. When combined with technical analysis and risk management strategies, it enhances decision-making. By integrating fundamental analysis, traders navigate markets skillfully and pursue investment objectives with confidence.

Using Fundamental Analysis in Futures Trading

While technical analysis focuses on historical price patterns and chart behavior, fundamental analysis examines the underlying forces that influence price over time. Rather than asking, "What is price doing?" fundamental analysis asks, "Why is price moving?" This distinction is critical. Traders use it to assess factors influencing supply and demand dynamics in commodities, currencies, and financial instruments.

Fundamental analysis serves as a pivotal tool in futures trading, offering traders valuable insights into market dynamics, the intrinsic value of assets, and underlying economic factors (*Winvesta, 2022*). Unlike technical analysis, which primarily focuses on historical price data and market trends, fundamental analysis delves into the fundamental aspects of assets, encompassing economic indicators, industry trends, and company-specific factors (*Magnimetrics, 2022*).

Unlike stock investing, where company earnings and balance sheets are central, futures analysis often focuses on broader forces such as Production Levels, Inventory Data, Weather Patterns, Interest Rate Policy, Trade Flows, Currency Strength, Government Reports, etc. For instance, in agricultural futures, weather conditions and global demand impact prices, while in currency futures, interest rates and trade balances drive value.

In crude oil futures, OPEC production decisions and inventory reports move prices. In currency futures, interest rate differentials and trade balances drive valuation. In stock index futures, inflation data and Federal Reserve policy influence direction.

Another example, if inflation is persistently rising and the central bank signals rate hikes, interest rate futures and equity index futures may react before technical breakdowns occur. A trader aware of these macro shifts is less likely to be surprised by volatility.

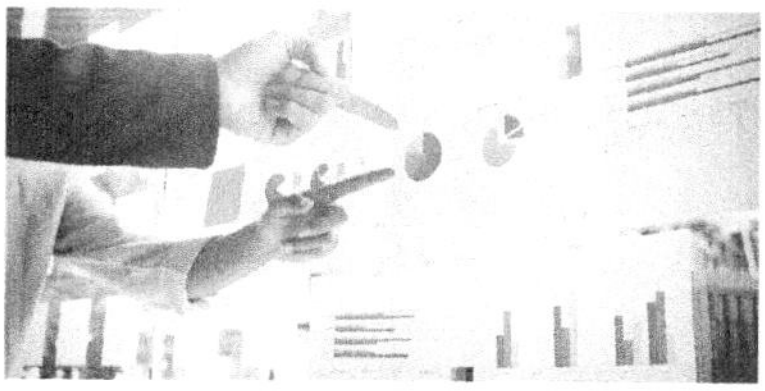

Figure 6.1: Analyzing futures market trends.

Importance and Benefits

Fundamental analysis offers several advantages in futures trading. By evaluating factors such as macro-level direction, identifying long-term trends, and anticipating volatility events and company financials, traders can gain a deeper understanding of market fundamentals and make informed trading decisions (*Nirmal Bang, 2022*).

Fundamental analysis enables traders to identify undervalued or overvalued assets, anticipate future trends, and mitigate risks associated with market volatility (*Investopedia, 2022*). It strengthens conviction in trade setups and reduces emotional trading driven by headlines. Fundamental analysis improves preparedness.

Methodologies and Approaches

Fundamental analysis encompasses various methodologies and approaches to evaluate the intrinsic value of assets. These methodologies and approaches can be typically described as three layers:

1. Macroeconomic Analysis

This type of analysis involves studying indicators such as the following:

- GDP growth
- Inflation (CPI, PPI)
- Employment data
- Interest rate decisions
- Central bank statements

These indicators influence currency, bond, and stock index futures. For example, higher-than-expected inflation often leads to rising interest rate expectations. This may cause bond futures to fall and equity futures to experience volatility.

2. Industry and Sector Analysis

Industry analysis involves examining trends and developments within specific sectors to identify growth opportunities and potential risks (*Strike Money, 2022*). Each futures contract is tied to a specific economic sector.

For commodities, traders examine:

- Production reports
- Inventory levels
- Seasonal cycles
- Export data
- Technological changes

For instance, in crude oil futures, weekly inventory reports from the U.S. Energy Information Administration (EIA) often cause sharp price reactions. Agricultural markets are highly seasonal and weather-sensitive. A drought forecast can drive prices upward before harvest data confirms shortages.

3. Supply and Demand Analysis

Supply and demand remain the ultimate drivers of futures prices. If supply decreases while demand remains constant, prices tend to rise. If supply increases while demand weakens, prices tend to fall. Understanding production cycles, global trade patterns, and storage capacity is crucial in commodity futures.

For example, if global copper production declines due to mine disruptions while infrastructure demand rises, copper futures may trend upward. Fundamental traders anticipate these imbalances early.

Factors Affecting Futures Prices

Futures prices, which serve as barometers of the expected values of underlying assets, are influenced by a range of factors, including supply and demand dynamics, market sentiment, macroeconomic indicators, and regulatory shifts. These elements interact in complex ways, shaping the pricing dynamics of futures contracts across diverse asset classes, including commodities, currencies, and financial instruments.

1. Supply and Demand Dynamics

Supply and demand form the foundation of futures pricing. Supply and demand fundamentals play a pivotal role in determining futures prices across diverse asset classes, including commodities, currencies, and financial instruments (*Groww, n.d.*).

Factors affecting supply include:

- Weather events

- Production disruptions
- Geopolitical conflict
- Regulatory changes

Factors affecting demand include:

- Economic growth
- Industrial activity
- Consumer behavior
- Energy consumption

2. Interest Rates

Changes in interest rates, driven by central bank policies and macroeconomic conditions, can impact borrowing costs, currency exchange rates, and investor sentiment (Investopedia, 2015). Interest rates significantly influence:

- Currency futures
- Bond futures
- Equity index futures

When central banks raise rates, borrowing becomes more expensive. This can slow economic growth and impact equity markets. Higher rates may strengthen a currency relative to others, affecting currency futures contracts. Interest rate expectations are often more important than the current rate itself.

3. Market Sentiment and Speculation

Futures markets are forward-looking. Investor sentiment, positioning, and expectations about the future often move markets before actual economic changes occur. Market sentiment and speculative activity contribute to fluctuations in futures prices as traders and investors react to news, events, and emerging trends (*Bajaj Finserv Securities, n.d.*).

Sentiment indicators such as the Commitments of Traders (COT) report offer insights into market sentiment and positioning, influencing trading decisions and price dynamics (*JSTOR, n.d.*).

Moreover, speculation by institutional investors and hedge funds can amplify price movements in futures markets, accentuating volatility and market dynamics (*Homework Study, n.d.*). Speculative positioning can amplify price swings, especially in highly leveraged markets. Traders must recognize that sentiment can temporarily override fundamentals.

4. Basis

Basis, defined as the difference between the spot and futures prices of an asset, reflects factors such as storage costs, interest rates, dividends, and supply-and-demand imbalances (*AgManager, n.d.*). A positive basis indicates that futures prices exceed spot prices, while a negative basis suggests the opposite (*CFFEX, 2010*).

Essentially, basis is the difference between the spot price and the futures price of an asset, which reflects:

- Storage costs
- Interest rates
- Time to expiration
- Supply-demand imbalances

If futures prices exceed spot prices, the market is said to be in contango. If futures prices are below spot prices, the market is in backwardation. Basis is particularly important for commodity traders and hedgers. Traders closely monitor basis levels to assess market conditions and arbitrage opportunities (*Extension Iowa State, n.d.*).

Futures prices are contingent on a range of variables, including supply and demand dynamics, interest rate fluctuations, market sentiment, speculative activity, and basis considerations. An in-depth understanding of these factors and their intricate interplay enables traders and investors to discern market trends astutely, pinpoint trading opportunities, and navigate risk skillfully in the dynamic realm of futures trading.

Incorporating Fundamental Analysis

Fundamental analysis empowers traders to make informed decisions, identify investment opportunities with favorable risk-reward profiles, and navigate financial markets with confidence and precision, positioning themselves for long-term success while minimizing exposure to undue risk.

Fundamental analysis strengthens low-risk trading by providing context. Low-risk strategies prioritize capital preservation and structured decision-making. When combined with fundamental analysis, traders avoid entering positions blindly.

For example, if economic data suggests slowing global growth, a trader may avoid aggressive long positions in industrial commodities until conditions stabilize. Fundamental awareness helps traders avoid fighting macro trends.

Real-World Macro Case Study

To understand how fundamental analysis operates in real time, consider a macroeconomic scenario in which inflation rises, and the central bank responds.

The Scenario: Inflation Surge

Assume inflation data (Consumer Price Index, CPI) begins rising consistently above central bank targets. Monthly CPI reports show inflation accelerating beyond expectations.

- What does this signal indicate?
- Rising consumer prices
- Decreasing purchasing power
- Increased probability of interest rate hikes
- Markets are forward-looking.
- Traders begin pricing in anticipated Federal Reserve tightening before the official announcement.

Impact Across Futures Markets

Bond Futures (Treasury Futures):
When inflation rises, interest rates are expected to increase. Bond prices move inversely to yields. That results in Treasury futures to decline.

Equity Index Futures (S&P 500, Nasdaq):
Higher interest rates increase borrowing costs and reduce corpo-

rate valuation multiples. This causes Equity Futures to experience volatility or downward pressure.

Currency Futures (U.S. Dollar Index):
Higher interest rates often strengthen a currency relative to others. These events may cause Dollar Futures to rise.

Commodity Futures (Gold):
Gold may initially rise as an inflation hedge, but it can decline if real interest rates increase significantly.

How a Fundamental Trader Responds

Instead of reacting emotionally after the rate hike announcement, a trader monitoring inflation trends

- Anticipates tightening policy early
- Avoids aggressive long equity positions
- Reduces exposure before CPI release
- Positions cautiously in Treasury futures
- Fundamental awareness provides preparation, not prediction.
- This is the difference between reacting and positioning.

Consider a commodity case study of crude oil futures.

The Scenario: Geopolitical Disruption

A major oil-producing region is experiencing geopolitical tensions that threaten supply disruption. Even before production numbers change, markets begin pricing in reduced future supply. Oil futures rise sharply.

A Fundamental Trader may evaluate current global inventory levels, OPEC production quotas, strategic petroleum reserve releases, and demand outlook. If inventories are already tight, the price response may be stronger and more sustained. If inventories are abundant, the spike may fade. Fundamental analysis allows the trader to assess whether the move is a temporary speculative move or structurally justified.

Step-by-Step Example:

This example depicts trading around a major economic report (CPI Release). Proper preparation transforms uncertainty into a structured opportunity. Let's walk through a disciplined approach.

Step 1: Identify the Event

Example: CPI report scheduled for 8:30 AM ET. Markets affected:

- Equity index futures
- Treasury futures

- Currency futures

Step 2: Understand Expectations

Markets move based on expectations versus actual results.

If expected inflation is 3.2% and actual comes in at 3.2%, price reactions may be minimal.

If the actual is 3.8%, volatility increases.

The deviation from expectation drives movement.

Step 3: Prepare Risk in Advance

Before the announcement:

- Reduce Position Size
- Tighten Stops
- Avoid new entries immediately before release
- Define Maximum Risk
- Volatility often spikes within seconds of release

Step 4: Observe Initial Reaction

After release, watch the first 1–5 minutes:

- Identify Direction
- Avoid Impulsive Entries
- Often, the first move is not the final move

Step 5: Align With Broader Context

If CPI confirms an existing macro trend (e.g., persistent inflation), continuation trades may develop. If CPI contradicts expectations, markets may reverse sharply. The key is not predicting the number, it is responding with discipline.

Example Trade Walkthrough

Assume CPI expected: 3.2%; CPI actual: 3.9% (higher than expected). Market Reaction:

- Treasury futures drop
- S&P futures fall
- Dollar futures rise

A trader focused on risk management may:

- Wait for initial volatility to settle (5–10 minutes).
- Enter short ES (S&P futures) once direction stabilizes.
- Place stop-loss above the pre-release high.
- Target logical support level.

Therefore, risk is defined before entry. Emotion is removed from execution. Fundamental awareness allows traders to choose when not to trade, which is often the most powerful decision.

Practical Integration Framework

To integrate fundamental analysis effectively, a series of basic questionnaires may help. Below is shown an example framework:

- **Begin with macro direction:**
  Are interest rates rising or falling? Is inflation accelerating?

- **Narrow to sector-specific drivers:**
  What supply reports or production changes are expected?

- **Align technical setups with fundamental bias:**
  Wait for chart confirmation rather than trading purely on news.

- **Adjust risk before major economic releases:**
  For example, reduce position size before Federal Reserve announcements.

Low-risk trading does not mean avoiding volatility. It means respecting it. When major macro events approach, a trader may:

- Reduce exposure.

- Avoid oversized positions.

- Use smaller contracts (such as micro futures).

Trade after confirmation rather than during chaos. Fundamental analysis guides positioning. Technical analysis times execution.

Common Mistakes in Using Fundamental Analysis

The intricate interplay of factors influencing futures prices underscores the dynamic nature of financial markets and the complexities involved in futures trading. Traders and investors must remain vigilant and proactive in monitoring supply and demand dynamics, market sentiment, macroeconomic indicators, and policy changes to stay ahead of market trends and make informed trading decisions.

By understanding the underlying drivers of futures prices and their interconnectedness, market participants can adapt their strategies, capitalize on emerging opportunities, and mitigate risks effectively.

Some of the common mistakes futures traders make using fundamental analysis:

- Trading headlines without context
- Ignoring market expectations versus actual data
- Overreacting to single data points
- Confusing short-term volatility with long-term trend

- Failing to manage risk despite strong conviction

Fundamentals can explain direction, but they do not eliminate risk.

Chapter Summary

Fundamental analysis equips traders with macro-level awareness that extends beyond price charts. By examining inflation trends, interest rate expectations, supply disruptions, inventory levels, and geopolitical developments, traders gain structured insight into the forces shaping futures markets.

Through real-world case studies such as inflation shocks and oil supply disruptions, we see how markets respond to shifts in economic reality. Understanding expectations, positioning, and macro drivers allows traders to anticipate volatility rather than react emotionally.

When integrated with technical confirmation and disciplined risk management, fundamental analysis becomes a strategic advantage, not for predicting the future, but for navigating it intelligently. In futures trading, preparation precedes precision. Understanding "why" price moves is as important as understanding "how" it moves.

The next chapter will build upon this foundation by exploring how to align fundamental insight with precise technical execution for structured trade planning.

Chapter Seven

Risk Management in Futures Trading

"A 10% decline in the market is fairly common, it happens about once a year. Investors who realize this are less likely to sell in a panic, and more likely to remain invested, benefitting from the wealth building power of stocks." - Christopher Davis

In leveraged markets where price movements can produce rapid gains or losses, the ability to control risk determines longevity. Traders who fail to prioritize risk management may experience temporary success, but rarely durability.

Risk management is paramount for success in futures trading, safeguarding capital, maintaining prosperity, and securing profitability. A disciplined risk management strategy entails careful planning, comprehensive analysis, and unwavering commitment to sound principles.

Understanding Market and Liquidity Risk

At its core, risk management involves identifying, evaluating, and controlling the potential risks that can impact trading positions and portfolios.

In futures trading, these risks include:

- **Market Risk:** Losses due to adverse price movements
- **Liquidity Risk:** Difficulty entering or exiting positions efficiently
- **Margin Risk:** Forced liquidation due to insufficient account equity
- **Operational Risk:** Errors in execution, system failure, or miscalculation

1. Market Risk

Market risk refers to the potential loss resulting from unfavorable price movement. Because futures are leveraged, even small percentage moves in the underlying asset can produce significant changes in account equity.

Futures markets respond rapidly to:

- Economic data releases
- Central bank policy changes

- Geopolitical events
- Supply disruptions
- Shifts in investor sentiment

2. Liquidity Risk

Liquidity describes how easily a contract can be bought or sold without significantly impacting price. It denotes how easily traders can enter and exit positions in the futures market without significantly affecting prices. Highly liquid futures contracts are generally easier to trade, while illiquid contracts may entail wider bid-ask spreads and increased price volatility.

Traders need to factor in liquidity when choosing futures contracts to trade, as contracts with low liquidity could present challenges during market exits, potentially resulting in unfavorable outcomes. Hence, managing liquidity risk is vital to mitigate situations where price fluctuations arise due to limited trading activity, thereby influencing the efficiency of risk management strategies.

Highly liquid contracts (such as ES, NQ, CL, or major currency futures) typically have:

- Tight bid-ask spreads
- Deep order books

- Faster execution

Illiquid contracts may exhibit the following:

- Wider spreads
- Slippage
- Increased volatility

Risk Management Techniques for Futures Trading

Traders adeptly employ an array of techniques and strategies, meticulously crafted to mitigate potential losses and optimize the delicate balance between risk and reward inherent in their trading endeavors. Here, we explore key risk management techniques for futures trading as outlined by industry experts and trading platforms:

1. Position Sizing

One fundamental risk management technique is position sizing (*NinjaTrader, n.d.*). This involves determining the appropriate size of each trading position relative to account size, risk tolerance, and market conditions. Traders allocate a predetermined percentage of capital to each trade, thereby limiting potential losses and managing overall portfolio risk.

Rather than asking, "How much can I make?" the disciplined trader asks, "How much can I afford to lose?" Position sizing prevents catastrophic loss from a single trade. A common structured approach entails:

- Risk 1–2% of account equity per trade
- Determine stop-loss distance first
- Calculate contract quantity based on allowable risk

Example:

Account size: $25,000

Risk tolerance: 1% per trade = $250

Stop distance: 5 ES points

ES value per point: $50

5 × $50 = $250 risk per contract

Result: Trade 1 contract

2. Emotional Discipline

Emotional discipline is another crucial aspect of risk management in futures trading, as emphasized by LinkedIn (*LinkedIn, n.d.*). Emotions such as fear and greed can cloud judgment and lead to impulsive decision-making. Traders must learn to manage emotions effectively, adhere to their trading plan, and exercise patience and discipline in executing trades. Risk management is as much psychological as mathematical.

- Fear leads to premature exits.
- Greed leads to oversized positions.
- Frustration leads to revenge trading.

Emotional discipline requires:

- Predefined entry and exit rules,
- Acceptance of loss as part of trading,
- Avoiding impulsive position increases.

3. Stop-Loss Orders

Investopedia highlights the importance of stop-loss orders as a risk management tool in futures trading. A stop-loss order is a predefined price level at which a trader exits a losing position, thereby limiting losses and protecting capital. Traders can set stop-loss orders based on predetermined risk tolerance levels and market conditions.

Stop-loss orders define maximum acceptable loss before entering a trade and help with the following:

- Limit Downside Exposure
- Prevent Catastrophic Drawdowns

- Remove Emotional Hesitation

Stops should be placed based on market structure, not arbitrary dollar amounts. However, traders must also recognize that in fast-moving markets, slippage can occur. A stop reduces risk; it does not guarantee execution at an exact price.

4. Diversification

Diversification is a fundamental risk management principle (*AvaTrade, n.d.*). By diversifying their portfolio across different asset classes, markets, and trading strategies, traders can reduce exposure to any single source of risk. Diversification spreads risk across multiple investments, helping to mitigate the impact of adverse market movements on the overall portfolio. However, true diversification requires low correlation.

Diversification should be strategic, not random. For example, trading ES and NQ simultaneously may not provide meaningful diversification, as both respond similarly to macro forces.

Better diversification may include exposure across:

- Equity Index Futures

- Commodity Futures

- Currency Futures

5. Risk Analysis and Monitoring

Sophisticated risk management tools and technologies play a pivotal role in monitoring and managing exposure effectively. Risk analytics software provides real-time data and metrics to assess portfolio risk, identify vulnerabilities, and implement mitigation strategies. Modern trading platforms provide tools to evaluate:

- Portfolio exposure
- Margin utilization
- Volatility sensitivity
- Correlation

Monitoring margin utilization is especially critical in leveraged markets. Maintaining unused buying power reduces the probability of margin calls. Robust risk management forms the foundation of prosperous futures trading ventures.

It entails a comprehensive strategy that harmonizes diverse techniques, strategies, and tools to mitigate losses while maximizing risk-adjusted returns. Position sizing, a fundamental component of risk management, enables traders to allocate capital judiciously, striking a delicate balance between risk and profit potential across their portfolio.

Through prudent position sizing, considering variables like account size, risk tolerance, and prevailing market conditions, traders can cushion against adverse market fluctuations and safeguard their capital amidst volatile periods.

Hedging Strategies to Minimize Risk

To hedge, in finance, is to take an offsetting position in an asset or investment that reduces the price risk of an existing position. A hedge is therefore a trade that is made to reduce the risk of adverse price movements in another asset. Normally, a hedge consists of taking the opposite position in a related security or in a derivative security based on the asset to be hedged.

Hedging serves as a prudent risk management technique deployed by investors and businesses to shield themselves from unfavorable price swings in financial markets. Essentially, it entails assuming a complementary position in a correlated asset or financial instrument to offset potential losses on current investments and reduce exposure to price movement.

In essence, hedging operates similarly to acquiring insurance for investment, offering assurance that losses are contained, regardless of adverse market shifts.

Hedging, as employed within the framework of futures trading, entails the strategic utilization of futures contracts to mitigate the potential repercussions of price fluctuations in underlying assets such as commodities, currencies, or securities. It is designed to reduce uncertainty.

1. Hedging vs Speculation

It is important to distinguish Hedging vs Speculation and clarify the differences. Many traders confuse the two. A hedge reduces volatility in overall portfolio performance. Speculation increases exposure. Understanding your intention before entering a trade clarifies risk structure.

- Speculation: Seeking profit from price movement

- Hedging: Reducing risk from existing exposure

2. Interest Rate Hedge

Consider a hypothetical scenario where a pension fund manager harbors concerns regarding the impact of ascending interest rates on the valuation of the fund's fixed-income holdings. If rates rise, bond prices fall. The fund may sell Treasury futures to hedge exposure. If rates increase, cash bond values decline. Short futures position gains and losses are offset by gains.

To proactively manage this risk, the manager opts to engage in hedging by selling futures contracts correlated with interest rates. Through this action, they establish a predetermined interest rate for forthcoming transactions, thereby fortifying the value of the fund's investments against potential downturns resulting from interest rate escalations.

Should interest rates indeed surge, any losses incurred in the cash market are counterbalanced by gains realized in the futures market, effectively shielding the fund's comprehensive investment portfolio from adverse movements in interest rates.

3. Commodity Hedge

Similarly, businesses engaged in commodity trade often use currency futures contracts to hedge against fluctuations in price. In this way, hedging allows businesses to focus on their core operations without being overly exposed to the uncertainties of currency markets.

Consider a scenario where a wheat farmer expects a harvest in three months but predicts falling prices. The farmer sells wheat futures at today's price. If market prices fall at harvest, the cash sale price decreases. Short futures position gains and income are stabilized.

4. Currency Hedge

Businesses engaged in international trade often use currency futures contracts to hedge against fluctuations in exchange rates. By entering into currency futures contracts to buy or sell foreign currency at a predetermined price, businesses can protect against the risk of adverse movements in exchange rates that could erode profits or increase costs.

For example, a company expecting payment in euros may buy euro futures to hedge currency risk if it expects dollar strengthening. Similarly, a multinational corporation may use currency futures to hedge against fluctuations in exchange rates, ensuring stable cash flows and minimizing the impact of currency volatility on its bottom line. Hedging allows businesses to stabilize cash flow and reduce uncertainty.

Options as Hedging Tools

Options serve as financial instruments providing the holder with the right, but not the obligation, to buy or sell an underlying asset at a predetermined price within a specified timeframe, commonly employed for hedging or speculative purposes. Options on futures provide additional flexibility.

In the futures market, options play a crucial role in managing risk and executing trading strategies. With options, traders can craft intricate trading strategies like spreads, straddles, and butterflies to optimize profitability while minimizing downside risks, solidifying their significance within the futures market ecosystem.

Put and Call

Options contracts represent a robust tool for hedging, enabling investors to shield their portfolios from unfavorable price shifts while retaining the ability to capitalize on potential upward movements. Put options, for instance, grant the holder the privilege to vend an asset at a predetermined price, effectively mitigating downside risk.

Buying a put option protects against downside risk. Conversely, call options serve as a safeguard against overlooked opportunities, affording the holder the entitlement to procure an asset at a predetermined price. Buying a call option protects against missed upside.

Unlike futures, options limit maximum loss to the premium paid. However, options introduce complexity such as time decay and implied volatility considerations.

Trading Strategies

Traders employ a variety of investment strategies tailored to their preferences and risk tolerance levels. Short-term traders focus on immediate market fluctuations, engaging in day trading or swing trading to capitalize on short-term price movements within hours or days.

On the other hand, long-term traders take a patient approach, investing in assets such as stocks, bonds, and real estate to achieve sustained growth over months, years, or even decades. In terms of trading styles, below are the traders' styles and psychology:

- Aggressive traders embrace higher risk levels in pursuit

of potentially greater returns through high-frequency trading, options, or leveraged investments.

- Passive traders prefer low-cost index funds or ETFs, holding onto investments for the long term to secure consistent returns without active management.
- Passive-aggressive traders strike a balance between aggression and passivity, diversifying strategies to manage risk while pursuing growth opportunities.
- Conservative traders prioritize capital preservation and risk aversion, favoring low-risk investments like government bonds and blue-chip stocks to maintain stability and security.

Managing Margin Requirements and Contract Sizes

Margin management is one of the most misunderstood aspects of futures trading. Margin is not the cost of the contract. It is a performance bond. Margin requirements denote the capital traders must deposit with brokers to initiate and sustain positions in futures contracts, while contract sizes delineate the quantity of the underlying asset each futures contract embodies.

Conjointly, adept management of margin requirements and contract sizes is indispensable for risk control, leveraging opportunities to the fullest extent, and refining trading efficacy.

Best Practices for Margin Management

Strategic risk management techniques, including thoughtful position sizing and diversification, serve as integral components in effectively managing margin requirements and contract sizes. Traders must refrain from overextending their positions by allocating a judicious portion of their trading capital to each trade. Survival requires a buffer.

Additionally, diversifying across various asset classes and contract types can mitigate risk exposure and minimize the repercussions of unfavorable price fluctuations on the entire trading portfolio. The recommendations are:

- Keep excess margin available
- Avoid using full buying power
- Monitor volatility changes
- Reduce size during uncertain macro events
- No trading at maximum allowable leverage

Through the implementation of disciplined risk management methodologies and unwavering attention to margin requirements and contract sizes, traders can confidently navigate the intricacies of futures markets and consistently work towards attaining their trading goals.

1. Initial vs Maintenance Margin

An essential facet of managing margin requirements is understanding the distinction between initial and maintenance margin. Initial margin denotes the initial deposit necessary to initiate a futures position, while maintenance margin signifies the minimum equity level mandated to be upheld in the trading account to avert a margin call.

- Initial Margin: Required to open a position
- Maintenance Margin: Minimum equity required to maintain it

Traders must ensure they have sufficient funds to meet initial margin requirements and maintain adequate equity levels to avoid margin calls, which could precipitate the forced liquidation of positions at disadvantageous prices. If account equity falls below the maintenance margin, a margin call occurs. Failure to meet margin requirements can result in forced liquidation.

2. Contract Size and Leverage

Traders must diligently evaluate contract sizes when devising their trading strategies. Contract sizes vary depending on the underlying asset, with each contract representing a specific quantity of the asset. Each futures contract represents a defined notional value.

For example, a single S&P 500 E-mini futures contract typically represents a notional value of $50 times the index level. This creates leverage. Leverage magnifies both profits and losses. Understanding contract size allows proper position scaling.

- S&P 500 at 5,000
- ES multiplier: $50
- Notional value: $250,000
- Yet the margin may be approximately $12,000.

For smaller accounts, micro futures (such as MES) allow more precise risk control.

Final Principles of Risk Management

Risk management is not a single tool. It is a structured discipline applied consistently. Implementing robust risk management practices is like having a safety net beneath your tightrope walk in the futures market. It is about keeping a cushion of funds handy to cover margin requirements and sticking to disciplined position sizing.

Moreover, derivatives such as swaps and forwards enable market participants to customize hedging strategies to suit their specific risk management needs. Interest rate swaps, for instance, allow borrowers to convert variable-rate debt into fixed-rate debt, protecting against rising interest rates.

Similarly, commodity forwards enable producers and consumers to lock in prices for future delivery, hedging against volatility in commodity markets. By keeping a close eye on your account equity, following risk management protocols, and staying updated on market shifts, you are not just weathering storms but also seizing profitable opportunities along the way.

As a final reminder, below is a good list to go by:

- Protect Capital First.

- Define Risk Before Entry.

- Never risk more than you can psychologically tolerate.

- Maintain a Margin Cushion.

- Adapt position size during volatility.

- Accept losses as an operational cost.

With a disciplined approach, a finger on the pulse of market dynamics, and savvy risk management strategies, you're not just trading; you're charting a course towards your financial goals in the futures market.

Chapter Summary

Leveraged markets reward preparation and punish excess exposure. Through disciplined position sizing, strategic use of stop-loss orders, diversification, margin awareness, and emotional control, traders can withstand volatility and preserve capital. Hedging strategies provide additional tools for mitigating risk across portfolios and business operations.

Understanding contract size and leverage ensures informed decision-making rather than accidental overexposure. At its core, risk management in futures trading hinges upon the astute recognition, evaluation, and mitigation of potential risks that could imperil trading positions and portfolios.

Market risk, liquidity risk, credit risk, and operational risk loom large as traders undertake a comprehensive assessment of diverse risks. For instance, market risk encompasses losses stemming from adverse movements in futures prices driven by economic indicators, geopolitical shifts, and supply-demand dynamics.

Conversely, liquidity risk poses challenges in executing trades or exiting positions due to insufficient market liquidity. Moreover, the utilization of sophisticated risk management tools and technologies, such as risk analytics software and automated orders, empowers traders to monitor and manage exposure effectively, thus fortifying their resilience in the face of market uncertainties.

Ultimately, profitability in futures trading is not determined by how much one can make in a single trade but by how effectively one can manage risk over hundreds of trades. Consistency, not aggression, defines long-term success.

Chapter Eight

Strategies, Strategies, Strategies!

"Waiting helps you as an investor and a lot of people just can't stand to wait. If you didn't get the deferred-gratification gene, you've got to work very hard to overcome that." - Charlie Munger

In the world of Futures Trading, success often hinges on the effectiveness of trading strategies. In previous chapters, we established the foundation: planning, psychology, market mechanics, technical analysis, fundamental analysis, and risk management.

This chapter builds upon that foundation by focusing on execution, the practical strategies traders use to participate in futures markets.

From building a comprehensive trading plan to employing strategies such as day trading, swing trading, trend following, scalping, and options trading, this chapter offers a detailed exploration of how traders can navigate the dynamic futures market landscape.

Futures Trading Strategies

A strategy is not simply a method of entering trades. It is a structured approach to capturing opportunity within a defined timeframe, under defined conditions, with controlled risk. Different traders succeed using different strategies.

The key is alignment between:

- Your Personality
- Your Time Availability
- Your Risk Tolerance
- Market Conditions

Building a Trading Plan

A trading plan stands as the compass guiding traders through the labyrinth of the financial markets, meticulously delineating their objectives, risk thresholds, entry and exit strategies, and overarching methodologies. **Trading Success Logbook**

While the mechanics of building a trading plan were covered earlier, strategy selection must align with your overall framework.

A strategy without structure becomes speculation. A structured strategy becomes repeatable.

Your trading plan should clearly define:

- Which strategy type do you use?
- When do you trade?
- Which contracts do you trade?
- What is your Risk-to-Reward Ratio?
- What is your maximum risk per trade?
- What are your Entry and Exit criteria?

Here are some important factors to consider in building a trading plan:

1. Define Your Objectives

The first step in building a trading plan is to define clear and achievable objectives (*Growthink, n.d.*). These objectives could include financial goals, such as achieving a certain level of profitability or building a consistent income stream from trading.

Additionally, traders should consider their risk tolerance and time commitment to trading, as these factors will influence their trading strategies and approach.

2. Risk Management Strategies

Effective risk management is a cornerstone of any successful trading plan (*ThinkMarkets, n.d.*). Traders must identify potential risks associated with their trading activities and implement strategies to mitigate them (*Nadex, n.d.*). Remember, within this book, there are chapters dedicated to this topic, emphasizing the importance of risk management. Chapter 7of this book is dedicated to this topic.

3. Trading Strategies and Techniques

A trading plan should outline the specific strategies and techniques that traders will use to enter and exit trades (*Axi, n.d.*). This may include technical analysis tools such as chart patterns, indicators, and oscillators, as well as fundamental analysis methods such as economic data releases and news events (*Tradeciety, n.d.*). Chapter 5goes through this extensively. Traders should also define their criteria for identifying trading opportunities and establish clear rules for trade execution based on their analysis.

4. Review and Adaptation

A trading plan is not static but should evolve over time based on changing market conditions and individual trading performance (*IG, n.d.*). Traders should regularly review their trading plan to assess its effectiveness and make necessary adjustments (Investopedia, 2004). This may involve refining trading strategies, updating risk management techniques, or incorporating new tools and resources to improve decision-making processes.

5. Discipline and Consistency

Perhaps the most crucial aspect of a trading plan is discipline and consistency in its execution (*Axi, n.d.*). Traders must adhere to the rules and guidelines outlined in their trading plan, even in the face of market volatility and uncertainty (*ThinkMarkets, n. d.*). By maintaining discipline and consistency, traders can avoid impulsive decision-making and emotional trading, which often lead to poor results in the long run (*Nadex, n.d.*).

Common Day Trading Strategies for Futures

Day trading involves opening and closing positions within the same trading session. No positions are held overnight. Trading epitomizes the art of executing trades within a single trading day, harnessing transient price movements for profit. In this dynamic realm, day traders rely heavily on technical analysis, intraday price action, chart patterns, and momentum indicators to pinpoint opportune moments.

This strategy appeals to traders who:

- Prefer active engagement,

- Have time during market hours,
- Seek short-term opportunities,
- Want to avoid overnight risk.

1. Trend Trading (Intraday)

One common strategy for day trading futures is trend trading (*TastyLive, n.d.*). Traders identify prevailing trends in the market and enter positions in the direction of the trend. For example, if the market is in an uptrend, traders look to buy contracts, while in a downtrend, they seek short-selling opportunities.

Trend traders rely on technical indicators such as moving averages and trendlines to confirm market direction and identify potential entry and exit points (*Quantified Strategies, n.d.*). In intraday trend trading, traders identify directional momentum within the session. Intraday trend trading works best in volatile, directional markets.

Example:

- The market opens strong above the prior high.
- Volume increases.
- Pullbacks are shallow.

The trader enters in the direction of momentum and exits before the session closes.

2. Range Trading

Range trading focuses on markets oscillating between support and resistance during the session. Range Traders aim to buy at support and sell at resistance, profiting from the price movements within the range. Range trading requires patience. This strategy works best during low-volatility or consolidation sessions. and discipline, as traders wait for clear signals indicating potential breakouts or reversals within the established range (*Bookmap, n.d.*).

To summarize, Range Traders:

- Buy near support.
- Sell near resistance.
- Exit when range breaks.

3. Scalping

Scalping is a high-frequency trading strategy commonly used in day trading futures (*LinkedIn, n.d.*). Traders capitalize on small price movements by entering and exiting positions rapidly, often within seconds or minutes. Scalpers aim to capture multiple small gains throughout the trading session, relying on tight spreads and quick execution to generate profits.

This strategy requires advanced technical analysis skills, fast internet connectivity, and robust risk management practices to mitigate losses (*Jigsaw Trading, n.d.*). Scalping is an ultra-short-term form of day trading. Transaction costs and slippage must be carefully managed, as they can erode profitability.

In summary, in scalping, traders:

- Hold positions for seconds to minutes.
- Target small price movements.
- Execute multiple trades per session.

Scalping requires high liquidity, tight spreads, fast execution, and emotional control.

Swing Trading Strategies for Futures

Swing trading strategies are finely tuned to capture the undulating price movements within the overarching market trend, spanning short to medium terms. Traders embracing swing trading methodologies maintain positions for periods ranging from several days to weeks, strategically aligning with the oscillations of market sentiment to capitalize on emerging opportunities.

These strategies often incorporate technical analysis tools such as moving averages, trendlines, and Fibonacci retracements to identify potential entry and exit points. Swing traders focus on broader price structure rather than intraday noise.

This strategy appeals to traders who:

- Have full-time jobs,
- Cannot monitor markets constantly,
- Prefer capturing intermediate trends,
- Are comfortable holding overnight positions.

Common Swing Trading Tools

1. Moving Averages

One common swing trading strategy involves using moving averages to identify trend reversals and entry points (*Forbes, n.d.*). Traders often look for crossover signals between short-term and long-term moving averages, such as the 50-day and 200-day moving averages, to confirm the beginning of a new trend.

Moving averages help traders filter out market noise and focus on significant price movements, enabling them to capitalize on trend reversals effectively. Swing traders often use moving averages to help filter the noise and identify structural trend direction.

For example:

A rising 50-day moving average confirms upward bias.

Pullbacks to moving average may offer entry opportunities.

2. Support and Resistance

Another key aspect of swing trading strategy is the identification of support and resistance levels (*Schwab, n.d.*). Traders analyze historical price data to identify key price levels where the market has previously reversed direction.

By entering trades near support levels in uptrends or resistance levels in downtrends, traders aim to capitalize on potential price bounces or breakouts. Support and resistance define risk clearly, and swing traders identify historical price levels where markets previously reversed.

Entries are often taken:

- Near support in uptrends
- Near resistance in downtrends
- On breakouts from consolidation.

3. Momentum Indicators

Swing traders often utilize technical indicators such as the Relative Strength Index (RSI) and the Moving Average Convergence

Divergence (MACD) to confirm trade signals and gauge market momentum (*Optimus Futures, n.d.*). These indicators help traders assess whether a market is overbought or oversold and identify potential trend continuation or reversal points.

By combining multiple technical indicators and analyzing their signals in conjunction with price action, swing traders can make well-informed trading decisions and increase the probability of successful trades. Indicators are confirmation tools, not standalone systems.

For example:

RSI showing bullish divergence may signal reversal.

MACD crossover may confirm a momentum shift.

Trend-Following Strategies for Futures

Trend-following strategies entail the identification and harnessing of momentum within established market trends. Traders employing these strategies seek to leverage prolonged price movements aligned with the prevailing trend direction. They often utilize trend indicators like moving averages or the Average Directional Index (ADX) to validate trend direction and sift through market noise effectively.

Trend following differs from swing trading in that it seeks to capture extended directional movement, sometimes lasting months. This strategy works well in strongly trending markets, such as commodities during supply shocks or equity futures during sustained bull or bear phases.

Trend followers:

- Do not predict reversals
- Follow established direction
- Allow profits to run
- Accept multiple small losses

Trend-following strategies for futures offer traders a systematic approach to capitalize on sustained price movements in the market (*FasterCapital, n.d.*). Just like swing trading, common tools for trend following include moving average crossovers, breakout systems, and volatility-based trailing stops. Trend following requires patience and psychological resilience.

1. Moving Averages

Traders often use simple moving averages (SMA) or exponential moving averages (EMA) to identify the direction of the trend. A common strategy involves looking for crossovers between short-term and long-term moving averages, such as the 50-day and 200-day SMAs. When the short-term moving average crosses above the long-term moving average, it may signal an uptrend, while a cross below may indicate a downtrend.

2. Trendline Breakouts

Another trend-following strategy involves identifying trendline breakouts (*TradeCiety, n.d.*). Traders draw trendlines connecting consecutive swing highs or swing lows to visualize the direction of the trend. When the price breaks above a downward trendline or below an upward trendline, it may signal a potential trend reversal. Traders can enter positions in the direction of the breakout and ride the trend until signs of exhaustion or reversal appear.

3. Momentum Indicators

Momentum indicators help traders assess the strength of a trend and identify potential overbought or oversold conditions. When the RSI or MACD shows divergence from price movements, it may indicate a weakening trend and potential reversal. Trend followers use these signals to adjust their positions or exit trades to lock in profits.

Scalping Strategies for Futures

While scalping was introduced under day trading, it deserves separate emphasis. Scalping strategies focus on capitalizing on small price movements in the market by executing rapid-fire trades with tight profit targets and stop-loss levels. As explained earlier, scalpers aim to capture small profits consistently throughout the trading session while minimizing exposure to market risk.

Scalping depends heavily on:

- Order Flow Awareness
- Market Depth
- Patience and Consistency
- Execution Speed
- Strict Discipline

It is generally best suited for highly liquid contracts such as ES (S&P 500), NQ (Nasdaq), and CL (crude oil). Speed, precision, and discipline are key elements of successful scalping strategies in futures trading:

1. Timeframes and Chart Analysis

Scalping strategies often utilize short timeframes, such as one-minute or five-minute charts, to identify rapid price movements (*TradePro Academy, n.d.*). Traders focus on technical indicators such as moving averages, support and resistance levels, and volume to pinpoint entry and exit points. By closely monitoring price action and market depth, scalpers can capitalize on micro-level fluctuations in futures prices.

2. Order Flow and Market Liquidity

Successful scalping relies on ample market liquidity and tight bid-ask spreads (*Benzinga, n.d.*). Scalpers seek to execute trades in highly liquid futures contracts to minimize slippage and ensure fast order execution. They monitor order flow and market depth using Level II quotes to gauge supply and demand dynamics, identifying potential trading opportunities based on order imbalances and price momentum.

3. Risk Management and Trade Execution

Scalpers typically employ tight stop-loss orders to limit downside risk and exit losing trades quickly. They also implement proper position sizing techniques to manage capital efficiently and avoid overexposure to market volatility. Trade execution speed is paramount in scalping, with traders utilizing direct market access (DMA) platforms and advanced order types to execute trades with minimal latency (*IG, n.d.*).

Options Strategies in Futures Markets

Options on futures provide flexibility beyond directional trades. Options trading strategies offer traders a versatile toolkit for managing risk and capitalizing on market opportunities in futures markets. These strategies include buying and selling options contracts outright, as well as more complex strategies like straddles, strangles, and spreads.

Options provide traders with the flexibility to hedge against price fluctuations, generate income, and speculate on market movements with defined risks. According to Motilal Oswal Financial Services Limited (2021), options strategies offer flexibility and versatility, allowing traders to adapt to various market conditions and achieve their investment objectives. Unlike futures, options limit maximum loss to the premium paid (for buyers). They allow traders to:

- Hedge Futures Positions
- Define Maximum Risk
- Profit from Volatility
- Structure Neutral Strategies

Here are some of the strategies:

1. Protective Put Strategy

The protective put strategy involves purchasing a put option on an underlying asset to hedge against potential downside risk. If the asset's price declines, the put option provides the right to sell the asset at the predetermined strike price, thereby limiting losses

(Forbes, 2023). A trader long futures may purchase a put option to limit downside risk. This functions like insurance.

2. Covered Call (on Futures Equivalent)

A trader long futures may sell call options to generate income, though upside becomes capped.

Advanced Options Strategies

1. Long Straddle

In this scenario, traders may:

- Buy a call and a put at the same strike.
- Profits from large movement in either direction.
- Used when volatility is expected.

2. Iron Condor

In this strategy, traders may:

- Sell out-of-the-money call and put spreads.
- Profits when price remains within a defined range.
- Used in low-volatility conditions.

3. Vertical Spreads

In this case, traders may:

- Bull Put Spread (bullish bias),
- Bear Call Spread (bearish bias),
- These define risk while positioning directionally.

Options strategies add complexity and require understanding of implied volatility and time decay. They are powerful but should be approached methodically.

Choosing the Right Strategy

Not all strategies suit all traders.

Ask yourself:

- Can I monitor markets during the day?
- Am I comfortable holding overnight risk?
- Do I prefer fast action or patience?
- How do I respond to losing streaks?

For example:

A full-time professional may find swing trading more realistic than scalping.

A trader with limited capital may prefer micro futures combined with defined-risk options.

Strategy selection is not about prestige. It is about sustainability.

Strategy and Risk Integration

- Every strategy must operate within the risk framework discussed in Chapter 7.
- No strategy compensates for poor risk management.
- Position sizing, margin awareness, and discipline remain constant across all methods.
- Strategy determines opportunity.
- Risk management determines survival.

Strategy Comparison Matrix

To simplify strategy selection, the following comparison helps traders understand how each approach differs in terms of time commitment, risk exposure, and suitability. This makes it easier to align a strategy with personal goals, availability, and trading style.

TRADING STRATEGIES COMPARISON

STRATEGY	TIME REQUIRED	RISK LEVEL	BEST FOR	KEY STRENGTH	MAIN CHALLENGE
Day Trading	High (1–3 hrs/day)	Medium–High	Traders with flexible schedules	Fast feedback, many opportunities	Emotionally intense; requires focus.
Swing Trading	Low–Medium (30–60 min/day)	Medium	Working professionals	Less screen time; structured	Requires patience during slow markets.
Trend Following	Low (15–30 min/day)	Low–Medium	Beginners & side-hustle traders	Simple, rules-based	Long periods of waiting.
Scalping	Very High (constant monitoring)	High	Advanced traders	Frequent small wins	High stress; requires speed.
Breakout Trading	Medium	Medium	Active traders	Clear entry signals	False breakouts common.
Mean Reversion	Medium	Medium–High	Experienced traders	High reward potential	Requires precise timing.
Options Strategies	Medium	Variable	Traders seeking flexibility	Income generation & hedging	More complex to learn.

Figure 8.1: Strategy Comparison Matrix

Chapter Summary

Chapter 8 explored the structured approaches traders use to engage futures markets. From active intraday strategies such as trend trading, range trading, and scalping to broader swing and trend-following approaches, traders have multiple paths available. Options strategies further expand the toolkit, allowing for defined-risk positioning and volatility-based opportunities.

However, strategy alone does not guarantee success. Alignment between personality, timeframe, and risk tolerance is critical. When combined with disciplined execution and structured risk management, these strategies become repeatable systems rather than speculative attempts. Mastery of futures trading lies not in constant action but in structured decision-making applied consistently over time.

Chapter Nine

Advanced Trading Techniques

"Far more money has been lost by investors trying to anticipate corrections, than lost in the corrections themselves." - Peter Lynch

As traders progress beyond foundational knowledge, strategy design, risk control, psychology, and market mechanics, the edge shifts. At advanced levels, performance is no longer determined by discovering new indicators or adding complexity. Beyond mere functionality, factors such as reliability, speed of execution, and access to markets play pivotal roles in shaping traders' experiences and outcomes.

It is determined by refinement, execution quality, infrastructure reliability, and measured improvement. From market orders to advanced algorithmic techniques, traders navigate a diverse array of options to optimize their trade execution processes.

In this chapter, we bring together the structural components that transform a capable trader into a professional one: choosing the right institutional access, validating strategies through structured testing, executing with precision, and building a disciplined review framework that compounds improvement over time.

Choosing the Right Platform to Trade

Selecting the right trading platform is paramount for traders seeking to execute their strategies efficiently and effectively. Factors to consider include user interface, reliability, speed of execution, availability of technical analysis tools, and access to markets and asset classes. Traders should also evaluate pricing structures, including commissions, fees, and margin rates, to ensure they align with their trading frequency and volume.

Whether opting for a desktop, web-based, or mobile platform, traders must prioritize functionality, security, and ease of use to optimize their trading experience. Let's explore insights from various reputable sources to elucidate the process of choosing the optimal trading platform.

1. Understand Your Needs and Goals

Before selecting a trading platform, it's imperative to assess your trading needs and goals. There are factors such as trading frequency, asset classes of interest, and desired features. Understanding your requirements will help narrow down the options and prioritize platforms that align with your objectives (*Altus Financial, n.d.).*

2. Evaluate User Interface and Experience

The user interface plays a pivotal role in the trading experience. IG (n.d.) emphasizes the importance of a user-friendly interface that facilitates intuitive navigation and efficient trade execution.

A clutter-free layout, customizable dashboard, and easy access to essential tools and features contribute to a seamless trading experience. This enhances decision-making speed and helps traders respond more effectively to fast-moving market conditions.

3. Assess Reliability and Security

Reliability and security are paramount considerations when choosing a trading platform. It is important to select a platform with robust security measures to safeguard sensitive information and ensure the integrity of transactions.

Additionally, traders should assess the platform's uptime, outage history, and backup systems to mitigate the risk of disruptions during critical trading periods (*OANDA, n.d.*). Reliable system performance ensures uninterrupted access to markets, especially during high volatility sessions.

4. Consider Access to Markets and Instruments

The breadth of available markets and financial instruments is a critical factor for traders with diverse investment interests. Evaluate the range of assets offered by a trading platform, including stocks, forex, commodities, and cryptocurrencies. A platform that provides access to a comprehensive array of markets empowers traders to explore various opportunities and diversify their portfolios (*Outlook India, n.d.*).

5. Review Pricing and Fees

Pricing structures and fees can significantly impact trading costs and profitability. Carefully review commission rates, spreads, overnight financing charges, and other fees associated with trading on a platform. Transparent pricing and competitive rates ensure that traders can optimize their returns without being burdened by excessive costs (*CFI Financial, n.d.*).

The Structural Foundation: Exchanges and Brokers

Every futures trade begins with the exchange. Exchanges are the regulated marketplaces where contracts are listed and cleared. Brokers are the institutions that provide you access to those exchanges. Understanding this distinction matters because your broker determines how efficiently and reliably you access the exchange. The majority of global futures volume flows through major exchange groups.

In the United States, they are CME Group (which includes CME, CBOT, NYMEX, and COMEX), Intercontinental Exchange (ICE), and Cboe Futures Exchange (CFE). In Europe, they are Eurex and ICE Futures Europe. In the Asia-Pacific region, they are the Singapore Exchange (SGX), Hong Kong Exchanges (HKEX), Japan Exchange Group / Osaka Exchange, and the National Stock Exchange of India (NSE).

Similarly, there is the ASX 24 in Australia and the B3 in Brazil, and so on. When you trade contracts such as ES, MES, NQ, MNQ, CL, GC, or ZN, you are trading instruments listed on these exchanges. However, individual traders typically do not connect directly to exchanges. They open accounts with regulated brokerage firms that route their orders to those venues.

In the United States, prominent brokerage institutions offering futures access include:

- Interactive Brokers (IBKR)
- Charles Schwab (via thinkorswim)
- NinjaTrader
- AMP Futures
- Optimus Futures

In the United Kingdom and Europe:

- Interactive Brokers (regional entities)
- Saxo Bank
- City Index (StoneX)
- TradeStation Global
- TastyTrade (where regionally available)
- IG Group

Similarly, in Australia, there are Interactive Brokers Australia and ASX participant brokers for ASX 24 contracts.

The purpose of naming these institutions is not to endorse one over another but to illustrate that infrastructure choice matters. Margin policies, data quality, platform stability, and order functionality vary across firms. These variables affect slippage, execution speed, and risk transparency, especially during high-volatility periods.

An advanced trader evaluates a broker not by marketing promises but by regulatory oversight, margin structure clarity, availability of micro-contracts, platform stability under stress, order control features (brackets, OCO, and trailing stops), and transparent fee structure. At higher levels of trading, operational reliability is part of risk management.

Micro Futures and Precision Positioning

One of the most meaningful advancements in recent years has been the introduction of micro futures contracts. Micro contracts allow precision risk control. They enable traders to scale position sizes gradually, manage drawdowns responsibly, and align exposure with account size. Advanced trading is not about maximizing size. It is about optimizing risk efficiency.

For example, consider the S&P 500, where an E-mini (ES) contract moves $50 per index point and a Micro E-mini (MES) contract moves $5 per index point. If your stop is 10 points wide, then one ES contract risks $500, and one MES contract risks $50.

1. BackTesting: Validating Logic Before Risking Capital

Backtesting entails scrutinizing a trading strategy through historical market data to evaluate how a strategy would have performed under past conditions. Through simulating trades and scrutinizing past outcomes, traders gain valuable insights into the strategy's efficacy, refine parameters, and enhance performance.

Leveraging dedicated backtesting software and platforms, traders can assess numerous strategies across diverse market scenarios, timeframes, and asset categories, facilitating data-informed decision-making and ongoing enhancement. At advanced levels, strategies are not adopted because they "look good." They are tested.

Backtesting allows traders to simulate trades and assess how the strategy would have performed under past market conditions. By analyzing historical data, traders gain insights into the strategy's strengths and weaknesses, helping them make informed decisions about its viability in live trading environments (*Quantified Strategies, n.d.*).

Backtesting reveals:

- Win rate
- Average win versus average loss
- Maximum drawdown
- Sensitivity to volatility regimes
- Dependency on rare outlier events
- Suppose a trader designs a breakout strategy:
- Enter long when the price exceeds the prior week's high.
- Place a stop below the prior week's low.
- Target 2R or trail with volatility.

Without testing, the strategy may appear strong. But historical analysis may reveal that it only performs during strong macro-trending periods and fails in consolidation environments. The goal of backtesting is not to guarantee the future. It is to eliminate weak structures before capital is exposed.

2. Optimization Without Overfitting

Optimization involves refining trading strategies to maximize returns and minimize risks. Optimization is the process of adjusting parameters within a trading strategy to improve its performance (*Investopedia, n.d.*). By fine-tuning parameters such as entry and exit criteria, position sizing, and risk management rules, traders can optimize their strategies to adapt to changing market conditions and enhance profitability.

Optimization strategies aim to improve trading performance by refining key parameters within a trading strategy. Systematically adjusting parameters based on historical data to optimize strategy performance is important. Through iterative testing and refinement, traders can identify optimal parameter values that maximize returns while minimizing risks (*Keystone Strategy Trading, n.d.*).

Optimization refines parameters, but it must be approached carefully. Overfitting occurs when parameters are tuned so precisely to historical data that performance collapses in live trading.

A system that requires exact moving average lengths and narrowly defined thresholds is fragile. The objective is not perfection; it is durability.

Robust systems:

- Use simple rule sets.
- Perform reasonably across multiple environments.
- Survive small parameter variations.
- Show consistent risk-adjusted returns.

3. Execution: Where Theory Meets Reality

Order execution is the process of completing a trade based on the instructions provided by the trader. Order execution involves matching buy and sell orders in the market to facilitate the exchange of securities.

The execution process ensures that trades are conducted promptly and at the best available prices, minimizing slippage and maximizing efficiency (*Investopedia, n.d.*). Execution strategies are techniques employed by traders to optimize trade execution and achieve desired outcomes. Selecting appropriate execution strategies based on market conditions and trading objectives is paramount.

Common execution strategies include time-weighted average price (TWAP), volume-weighted average price (VWAP), and implementation shortfall, each designed to minimize market impact and achieve efficient trade execution (*CMC Markets, n.d.*). Even the strongest strategy can underperform if execution is sloppy.

Execution determines the following:

- Slippage
- Fill quality
- Emotional interference
- Risk containment
- Understanding order types is essential.

Effective execution is critical for translating trading ideas into profitable trades. Traders must understand various order types and execution strategies to execute trades efficiently while minimizing slippage and market impact.

Market orders, limit orders, stop orders, and advanced order types such as fill-or-kill and iceberg orders offer traders flexibility and control over trade execution. Additionally, employing algorithmic trading techniques allows traders to automate trade execution based on predefined criteria, optimizing entry and exit points, and mitigating emotional biases.

A market order guarantees participation but not price. A limit order guarantees price but not participation. A stop order activates at predefined levels. A stop-limit order adds price control. More advanced traders rely heavily on bracket orders. These automatically attach a stop-loss and target to an entry order. Once filled, risk is defined and mechanically enforced.

For example, if a trader buys 1 MES at 5,000 and stops at 4,990 with a target at 5,020, the system executes according to plan, removing emotional hesitation or improvisation. Advanced traders automate discipline wherever possible.

4. Monitoring and Reviewing Trades

It is imperative for traders to uphold detailed trade journals, logging entry and exit points, the rationale behind each trade, risk management parameters, and subsequent outcomes. Trading Success Logbook.

Consistent scrutiny of trade journals and performance metrics empowers traders to assess the efficacy of their strategies, pinpoint areas necessitating refinement, and adapt their methodologies correspondingly. Leveraging trading analytics tools and performance dashboards equips traders with actionable insights, empowering them to refine their performance and realize their trading goals. These tools help identify strengths and weaknesses in trading behavior, enabling continuous strategy improvement.

Regular Monitoring of Trading Strategies

Regular monitoring of trading strategies is essential for traders to stay informed about the performance of their trades and identify areas for improvement. Monitoring trading strategies regularly to assess their effectiveness and adapt to changing market conditions is paramount.

By analyzing key performance metrics such as win rate, risk-reward ratio, and maximum drawdown, traders can gain insights into the strengths and weaknesses of their strategies (*FasterCapital, n.d.*).

Analysis of Trade Performance

Analyzing trade performance involves evaluating the outcomes of individual trades and identifying factors contributing to success or failure. Track trade parameters such as entry and exit points, trade duration, and profit/loss to assess trade performance objectively.

By conducting a thorough analysis of trade data, traders can identify patterns, trends, and recurring mistakes, enabling them to refine their strategies and enhance overall performance (*Opt ionsTrading.org, n.d.*). This data-driven approach improves decision-making by highlighting what consistently works and what leads to losses. Over time, it supports more disciplined trading by reducing emotional bias and reinforcing proven strategies.

Importance of Trade Monitoring and Reviews

Trade monitoring and reviews are integral to maintaining discipline and accountability in trading. Regularly reviewing trade outcomes to learn from past experiences and avoid repeating costly mistakes is a good practice. Through systematic trade reviews, traders can identify areas for improvement, refine risk management practices, and develop greater self-awareness and emotional control (*Fidelity, n.d.*).

Utilizing Trading Performance Tools

Utilizing trading performance tools can streamline the process of monitoring and reviewing trades, providing traders with valuable insights and analytics. Leveraging trading performance analysis tools to track key metrics, visualize trade data, and identify performance trends over time is a must. These tools enable traders to make data-driven decisions and optimize their trading strategies for improved results (*Forex Academy, n.d.*).

Implementing a Feedback Loop

Implementing a feedback loop is essential for continuous improvement in trading. By reflecting on past performance, adjusting strategies accordingly, and setting clear objectives for future trades, traders can iterate and refine their approach over time, ultimately enhancing their overall trading success (*Oter App, n.d.*).

Slippage and Volatility Awareness

As discussed in the previous chapter, slippage increases during major economic reports, thin liquidity conditions, sudden momentum spikes, etc. Professional traders manage this by reducing size during high-impact news, avoiding market orders in unstable conditions, favoring highly liquid contracts, and tracking average slippage per contract. Execution efficiency compounds over time. Poor fills erode expectancy.

Awareness and Professional Boundaries

The defining characteristic of advanced traders is structured review. Each trade becomes data. A comprehensive journal record may include Setup Category, Entry and Exit Logic, Stop and Target Placement, R-Multiple Result, Slippage, Market Regime, Emotional State, Tracking Performance in R (risk units) standardizes results regardless of contract size. A weekly review using Trading Success Logbookmay include identifying the highest expectancy setups, measuring adherence to the plan, quantifying drawdown, and detecting recurring behavioral errors.

Advanced traders define limits before markets test them. They establish Maximum daily loss, Maximum weekly drawdown,

Reduced size protocols after drawdown, and "do not trade" conditions (fatigue, emotional stress, major uncertainty). These boundaries protect longevity. Longevity is the real competitive advantage.

As a final refinement and reminder, traders should practice simplicity over complexity. Complex systems often conceal inconsistency. Clarity produces consistency. If performance declines, professionals simplify.

- One primary market
- One timeframe
- One setup
- One risk rule

Chapter Summary

At advanced stages, trading success is no longer about discovering new strategies. It is about refinement. Reliable institutional access ensures stable execution. Micro contracts allow precision risk control. Backtesting validates structural integrity. Optimization strengthens durability. Execution discipline protects expectancy. Systematic review compounds improvement.

The advanced trader operates with infrastructure awareness, execution precision, and analytical humility. Success is not explosive. It is cumulative. From market orders to advanced algorithmic techniques, the chapter elucidates the nuances of trade execution, emphasizing the importance of minimizing slippage and maximizing efficiency.

Furthermore, the chapter advocates for a systematic approach to trade monitoring and review, where traders meticulously document trades and analyze performance metrics to glean insights and refine their approach over time.

In essence, Chapter 9 serves as a guiding beacon for traders navigating the complexities of advanced trading techniques. It offers a comprehensive roadmap for traders seeking to elevate their skills, optimize their processes, and thrive in the fast-paced world of financial markets.

Chapter Ten

AI and the Future of Futures Trading

"The real power of AI in trading is not replacing human judgment. It is enhancing disciplined decision-making."

Artificial Intelligence (AI) is rapidly transforming the world of finance and trading. What once required large institutional teams and expensive software is now becoming accessible to individual retail traders through affordable platforms, automated analysis tools, and intelligent market scanners.

However, despite the excitement surrounding AI, it is important to approach this topic with realism and discipline. AI is not a magical system that guarantees profits or predicts the market perfectly. Markets remain uncertain, emotional, and influenced by economic, geopolitical, and human behavioral factors. Effective use of AI requires combining its insights with sound risk management and critical human judgment.

Instead, AI should be viewed as a tool that can assist traders in:

- Organizing Information
- Reducing Manual Workload
- Identifying Patterns
- Improving Efficiency
- Supporting Structured Decision-Making

For working professionals balancing careers, families, and limited screen time, AI can become a powerful assistant when used responsibly.

What AI Can Actually Do in Futures Trading

AI systems are designed to process large amounts of information quickly. In futures trading, this can help traders:

- Scan multiple markets simultaneously.
- Identify technical patterns.
- Detect volatility changes.
- Summarize economic news.
- Automate alerts.

- Backtest strategies.
- Monitor risk exposure.

For example, instead of manually reviewing dozens of charts each evening after work, an AI-assisted platform may help identify:

- Breakout opportunities,
- Unusual volume activity,
- Moving average crossovers,
- Volatility spikes.

This can reduce screen time while helping traders remain organized and focused.

AI tools can also help reduce emotional overtrading. A rules-based alert system may prevent traders from impulsively entering random setups simply because they feel bored, anxious, or fearful of missing out. However, AI is still dependent on:

- Data quality,
- Programming logic,
- Historical assumptions,
- Market conditions.

AI can process information faster than humans, but it cannot eliminate uncertainty.

The Limitations of AI in Trading

Many online advertisements promote unrealistic expectations surrounding AI trading systems. Be cautious of any platform claiming guaranteed profits, "95% win rates," automatic wealth generation, or "zero risk" trading. No AI system can predict markets with certainty. Markets constantly change due to:

- Interest rate decisions,
- Inflation reports,
- Geopolitical events,
- Institutional flows,
- Economic recessions,
- Human emotional behavior.

An AI model trained during a trending market may fail during sideways volatility. A strategy that worked historically may suddenly stop performing. Additionally, AI systems can suffer from:

- Overfitting,
- Delayed reactions,

- Poor data quality,
- Technical failures,
- Internet outages,
- Incorrect assumptions.

AI should support decision-making, not replace personal responsibility and risk management.

AI-Assisted Workflow for a Working Professional

One of the greatest advantages of AI is helping traders organize their workflow efficiently, especially when balancing a full-time career and personal responsibilities.

Below is an example of a structured AI-assisted trading routine for a side-hustle futures trader.

Morning Preparation

Before work:

- Review AI-generated news summaries.
- Check economic calendar events.
- Identify high-volatility periods.
- Set price alerts on key futures contracts.

- Review support and resistance zones.

During Work Hours

Instead of staring at charts continuously:

- Receive automated alerts,
- Monitor price triggers,
- Review major market developments,
- Avoid emotional impulse trades.

Evening Review

After work:

- Review completed market movements,
- Journal trades,
- Analyze emotional decisions,
- Backtest setups,
- Study mistakes,
- Refine strategy rules.

This structured approach allows traders to remain engaged without allowing trading to consume their entire lives.

Popular Tools for Futures Traders

Below are several commonly used tools that may assist futures traders with analysis, automation, charting, and workflow management.

TradingView

As discussed in an earlier chapter, TradingView is one of the most popular charting platforms among retail traders.

Features include:

- Charting tools,
- Alerts,
- Technical indicators,
- Watchlists,
- Community ideas,
- Automated scripts.

TradingView offers both free and paid plans. The free version is often sufficient for beginners learning chart analysis and basic futures trading workflows.

Website: https://www.tradingview.com

NinjaTrader

NinjaTrader is widely used by futures traders and offers:

- Futures charting,
- Order execution,
- Strategy automation,
- Replay features,
- Simulation trading,

Many traders use NinjaTrader for futures market execution due to its integration with futures brokers and advanced trading tools. Simulation and paper trading modes may be available for free before funding a live account.

Website: https://ninjatrader.com

TrendSpider

TrendSpider focuses heavily on AI-assisted technical analysis.

Features include:

- Automated trendlines,
- Pattern recognition,
- Strategy testing,

- Market scanners.

This platform can help reduce manual chart analysis time.

Website: https://trendspider.com

QuantConnect

QuantConnect is designed for more advanced traders interested in:

- Algorithmic trading,
- Quantitative strategies,
- Python programming,
- AI model development.

This platform may be better suited for technically inclined traders with coding experience.

Website: https://www.quantconnect.com

Trade Ideas

Trade Ideas provides AI-assisted scanning and momentum analysis tools.

Features include:

- Real-time scanning,

- AI-generated trade ideas,
- Market momentum identification.

Some traders use this platform to identify high-activity opportunities quickly.

Website: https://www.trade-ideas.com

Understanding AI Trading Costs and Robo-Trade Fees

While many AI trading platforms advertise automation and advanced analysis, traders should understand the associated costs before subscribing. Common expenses may include:

- Monthly subscription fees,
- Exchange data fees,
- Broker commissions,
- API access charges,
- Automation platform fees,

Some platforms offer free versions with limited features, while others require monthly subscriptions ranging from approximately $20 per month to $50 per month to several hundred dollars per month for advanced institutional-grade tools.

Examples:

- TradingView offers a free version with optional upgrades.
- NinjaTrader simulation tools may be free for practice accounts.
- QuantConnect offers open-source and community features.

Some brokers provide free charting tools directly within their trading platforms. However, traders should avoid overspending on software before developing consistency. Expensive tools cannot replace discipline, risk management, or emotional control.

Many beginners mistakenly believe, "Better software automatically creates better trading." In reality, poor discipline with expensive software still produces losses, while disciplined execution with simple tools can produce steady improvement.

Automation Does Not Remove Risk

One dangerous misconception is believing automated systems eliminate trading risk. Even automated systems can fail due to

- Market volatility,
- Poor coding,

- Delayed execution,
- Internet outages,
- Slippage,
- Unexpected news events,
- Flawed assumptions,

A poorly designed trading bot can lose money faster than a manual trader because automation removes hesitation. For this reason, as discussed in Chapter 7 and Chapter 8, position sizing, stop-loss rules, and risk management remain essential even when using AI tools. Never allow automation to override your responsibility as a trader.

The Human Edge Still Matters

Despite advances in technology, successful trading still depends heavily on:

- Patience
- Emotional control
- Discipline
- Consistency

- Self-awareness

AI cannot fully understand:

- Your emotional state,
- Your financial responsibilities,
- Your stress levels,
- Your long-term personal goals,

As discussed in earlier chapters on psychology and risk management, emotional decision-making remains one of the greatest challenges in trading. Technology can assist your process, but self-management still determines long-term success.

Final Thoughts on AI and Futures Trading

Artificial Intelligence is reshaping financial markets and creating exciting opportunities for retail traders. When used responsibly, AI tools can improve efficiency, reduce screen time, support analysis, automate repetitive tasks, and help traders remain organized. However, AI should never replace discipline, structured risk management, emotional awareness, or realistic expectations

The most effective traders combine:

- Human judgment
- Emotional discipline

- Structured systems
- Intelligent technology

AI is not a shortcut to guaranteed profits. It is a tool that can support a thoughtful, disciplined, and sustainable trading process.

As futures markets continue evolving, traders who combine education, adaptability, emotional resilience, and responsible technology use may place themselves in a stronger position for long-term growth and financial empowerment.

Chapter Summary

This chapter offers a realistic perspective on the role of Artificial Intelligence (AI) in futures trading. It highlights how AI is making advanced trading tools accessible to retail traders, while also emphasizing that AI is not a guaranteed path to profit. The summary covers AI's benefits such as streamlining information, organizing workflows, identifying patterns, and supporting emotional discipline, while cautioning against overreliance and unrealistic expectations.

The text reviews several popular AI-assisted trading platforms and reminds readers that no software can substitute for discipline, sound risk management, and emotional self-control. It also addresses the risks and limitations of automated systems, reinforcing the importance of personal responsibility.

In conclusion, the chapter and the book underscore that successful trading relies on a blend of human judgment, emotional resilience, and responsible use of technology. This balanced approach is key to long-term growth and financial empowerment.

This marks the end of the book.

Appendices

Appendix A

Glossary of Futures Terminology

A

Ask Price

The lowest price a seller is willing to accept for a futures contract.

Arbitrage

The practice of profiting from price differences of the same asset in different markets.

B

Bear Market

A market condition where prices are consistently falling.

Bid Price

The highest price a buyer is willing to pay for a futures contract.

Breakout

When price moves strongly above resistance or below support, signaling a potential new trend.

C

Contract Size

The standardized quantity of the underlying asset in a futures contract.

Commodity

A raw material or primary agricultural product such as oil, gold, wheat, or natural gas.

Contango

A market condition where future prices are higher than the current spot price.

D

Day Trading

Opening and closing positions within the same trading day to avoid overnight risk.

Derivative

A financial instrument whose value is derived from an underlying asset.

E

Equity

The total value of a trader's account after accounting for profits and losses.

Expiry Date

The date on which a futures contract must be settled or closed.

F

Futures Contract

A standardized legal agreement to buy or sell an asset at a predetermined price on a future date.

Fill Price

The actual price at which an order is executed.

Fundamental Analysis

Analyzing economic, supply, and demand factors to predict price movement.

G

Gap

A price jump between two trading sessions where no trading occurs in between.

H

Hedging

A strategy used to reduce risk by taking an opposite position in the market.

L

Leverage

Using borrowed capital to control a larger position size in the market.

Limit Order

An order to buy or sell at a specific price or better.

Liquidation

Forced closing of a position due to insufficient margin.

M

Margin

The minimum amount of capital required to open and maintain a futures position.

Maintenance Margin

The minimum equity needed to keep a position open.

Market Order

An order executed immediately at the current market price.

Mark-to-Market

Daily adjustment of account balance based on unrealized profits or losses.

N

Noise (Market Noise)

Random price movements that do not reflect the overall trend

O

Open Interest

The total number of outstanding futures contracts that have not been closed.

Overnight Risk

The risk of price changes occurring while the market is closed.

P

Position

A trader's current exposure in the market (long or short).

Profit and Loss (P&L)

The financial gain or loss from a trade.

Pullback

A temporary reversal in price during a larger trend.

R

Resistance Level

A price level where selling pressure is strong enough to prevent further price increases.

Risk Management

The process of controlling potential losses using stop-losses, position sizing, and discipline.

Rollover

Transferring a position from an expiring contract to a later one.

S

Short Position

Selling a futures contract expecting the price to fall.

Slippage

The difference between expected price and actual execution price.

Spread

The difference between bid and ask price.

Stop-Loss Order

An order placed to automatically close a trade at a predefined loss level.

Support Level

A price level where buying pressure is strong enough to prevent further decline.

T

Take-Profit Order

An order that automatically closes a trade once a target profit is reached.

Technical Analysis

Analyzing charts, patterns, and indicators to predict price movements.

Tick Size

The minimum price movement allowed in a futures contract.

V

Volatility

The rate at which price moves up and down in the market.

Volume

The number of contracts traded during a specific period.

W

Whipsaw

A market condition where price quickly reverses direction, triggering false signals.

Appendix B

Prominent Futures Brokers (Retail Access)

United States

- Interactive Brokers (IBKR)
- Charles Schwab (thinkorswim)
- NinjaTrader
- AMP Futures

United Kingdom / Europe

- Interactive Brokers (regional entities)
- Saxo Bank
- TradeStation Global

- Tastytrade (availability varies)

Australia

- Interactive Brokers Australia
- ASX participant brokers

Appendix C

Major Futures Exchanges

United States

- CME Group (CME, CBOT, NYMEX, COMEX)
- Intercontinental Exchange (ICE)
- Cboe Futures Exchange (CFE)

Europe

- Eurex

- ICE Futures Europe

Asia-Pacific

- Singapore Exchange (SGX)
- Hong Kong Exchanges (HKEX)
- Japan Exchange Group / Osaka Exchange
- National Stock Exchange of India (NSE)
- ASX 24 (Australia)
- B3 (Brazil)

References

Regulatory & Institutional Authorities

- Commodity Futures Trading Commission. (n.d.). Educational resources and investor protection. https://www.cftc.gov/

- U.S. Securities and Exchange Commission. (n.d.). Investor education and financial literacy resources. https://www.sec.gov/

- CME Group. (n.d.). Futures market education and contract specifications. https://www.cmegroup.com/

Core Financial Education Platforms

- Investopedia. (n.d.). Futures trading overview. https://www.investopedia.com/futures/
- Investopedia. (n.d.). Futures contract definition and mechanics. https://www.investopedia.com/terms/f/futurescontract.asp
- Investopedia. (n.d.). Risk management in trading. https://www.investopedia.com/risk-management/
- The Motley Fool. (n.d.). Investment education and market analysis. https://www.fool.com/
- MarketWatch. (n.d.). Financial markets news and data. https://www.marketwatch.com/
- Investor.com. (n.d.). Investor education resources. https://www.investor.com/
- Liberated Stock Trader. (n.d.). Stock and futures trading education resources. https://www.liberatedstocktrader.com/

Learning Platforms & Online Courses

- Udemy. (n.d.). Futures trading and financial markets courses. https://www.udemy.com/

- 5paisa Finschool. (n.d.). Stock market education platform. https://www.5paisa.com/finschool/

Global Financial News & Media

- Bloomberg. (n.d.). Global financial news and analysis. https://www.bloomberg.com/
- CNBC. (n.d.). Live financial markets and business news. https://www.cnbc.com/
- Reuters. (n.d.). Global economic and financial reporting. https://www.reuters.com/
- Financial Times. (n.d.). International business and financial news. https://www.ft.com/
- The Wall Street Journal. (n.d.). Financial markets and economic reporting. https://www.wsj.com/
- Financial Post. (n.d.). Business and financial news coverage. https://financialpost.com/

Broker & Trading Education Resources

- Groww. (n.d.). Beginner trading guides and financial education blog. https://groww.in/blog/

- Angel One. (n.d.). Futures trading education and market insights. https://www.angelone.in/
- NinjaTrader. (n.d.). Futures trading tools and education. https://ninjatrader.com/
- OANDA. (n.d.). Technical analysis and trading guides. https://www.oanda.com/
- Warrior Trading. (n.d.). Day trading education resources. https://www.warriortrading.com/

Technical & Fundamental Analysis

- City Index. (n.d.). Introduction to technical analysis. https://www.cityindex.com/
- TrendSpider. (n.d.). Technical analysis strategies and tools. https://trendspider.com/
- OANDA. (n.d.). Technical analysis guide. https://www.oanda.com/
- Investopedia. (n.d.). Technical analysis overview and strategies. https://www.investopedia.com/technical-an

alysis/

- Investopedia. (n.d.). Fundamental analysis guide. https://www.investopedia.com/fundamental-analysis/
- NinjaTrader. (n.d.). Indicators and futures analysis tools. https://ninjatrader.com/

Futures Pricing & Market Structure

- CME Group. (n.d.). Futures pricing and market structure. https://www.cmegroup.com/
- Angel One. (n.d.). Futures pricing formula and concepts. https://www.angelone.in/
- Bajaj Finserv Securities. (n.d.). Factors influencing futures prices. https://www.bajajfinservsecurities.in/
- Investopedia. (n.d.). How futures prices are determined. https://www.investopedia.com/

Risk Management, Margin & Hedging

- CME Group. (n.d.). Margin and risk management in futures markets. https://www.cmegroup.com/

- NinjaTrader. (n.d.). Understanding margin in futures trading. https://ninjatrader.com/
- Investopedia. (n.d.). Hedging strategies and risk reduction. https://www.investopedia.com/hedging/
- Fidelity. (n.d.). Risk management and hedging strategies. https://www.fidelity.com/
- Corporate Finance Institute. (n.d.). Hedging and financial risk management. https://corporatefinanceinstitute.com/
- FasterCapital. (n.d.). Margin and risk management in futures trading. https://fastercapital.com/

Trading Strategies & Planning

- Investopedia. (n.d.). How to build a trading plan. https://www.investopedia.com/trading-plan/
- IG. (n.d.). Trading strategies and plan development. https://www.ig.com/
- Nadex. (n.d.). Building a structured trading plan. https://www.nadex.com/

- Axi. (n.d.). Trading plan and strategy resources. https:/ /www.axi.com/
- Tradeciety. (n.d.). Trading plan development guide. ht tps://tradeciety.com/

Risk, Strategy & Execution Insights

- Investopedia. (n.d.). Day trading strategies and execution. https://www.investopedia.com/
- Quantified Strategies. (n.d.). Systematic trading strategies research. https://www.quantifiedstrategies.com/
- Bookmap. (n.d.). Futures trading strategies and market behavior. https://bookmap.com/
- Jigsaw Trading. (n.d.). Order flow and trading strategies. https://www.jigsawtrading.com/

Made in the USA
Monee, IL
04 November 2026

67383093R00108